Never Say Old

Bartlett and Margaret Hess

While this book is designed for the reader's personal enjoyment and profit, it is also intended for group study. A Leader's Guide with Victor Multiuse Transparency Masters is available from your local bookstore or from the publisher.

VICTOR BOOKS a division of SP Publications, Inc.

WHEATON, ILLINOIS 60187

Offices also in
Whitby, Ontario, Canada
Amersham-on-the-Hill, Bucks, England

Recommended Dewey Decimal Classification: 601.435
   Suggested Subject Heading: GERONTOLOGY

Library of Congress Catalog Card Number: 84-50143
ISBN: 0-89693-375-X

VICTOR BOOKS
A division of SP Publications, Inc.
      Wheaton, Illinois 60187

CONTENTS

INTRODUCTION

Everybody wants to live a long time, but no one wants to be old. In some societies, old age is a disaster while in others it is the crown and climax of life. In our society, it can be either.

What can you do to determine the tone and temper of your life as the years add up? A good or a bad old age isn't something that just comes upon you. You can determine your interests, your activities, your friendships, your relationships and, to a large extent, even your health.

You can choose whether you will be a producer or a consumer. Producers are always welcome. Total consumers are a drag and a burden to society. Regardless of the state of your health or mobility, you can be wanted and desired.

This is a book for all ages—the young, the middle-aged, as well as the old. You can live creatively all your life.

Margaret and Bartlett Hess
Livonia, Michigan
1984

ONE ❧
ATTITUDES—
What Can You Do
About Them?

To know how to grow old is the master work of wisdom, and one of the most difficult chapters in the great art of living.

Amiel, Journal, Sept. 21, 1874

Margaret Hall is a youthful 67. She dresses stylishly, wears stunning hats, and keeps constantly busy at our church doing things like taking charge of luncheons for 500 people.

Margaret comments about some of the people on her block, "We've been blessed in our neighborhood. A woman across the street in her 80s is a world traveler—Europe, Hawaii, Alaska, the Carolinas. A neighbor who died at 92 worked in her son's jewelry store up to three days before. She polished silver, also coded and priced everything that came into the store.

"Two widows on this street are not active because they're not too well, but they manage alone.

"Mr. Stevens tuned pianos and sang in the choir till his late 90s. He lived alone, kept roomers. At 80 he painted his house. He died at 103.

"My mother lived with us till she died at 86. Her mind was as sharp as ever."

This is a whole new era for the old. An article in *U.S. News & World Report* (4 July 1983) quotes Dr. Roy Walford, authority on aging,

> We can already increase the maximum life span by dietary manipulation . . . before the end of this century—or even sooner—there will be easier ways to increase maximum life span so that people live to 150 years of age or more. I'm not saying that we can rejuvenate the body or reverse the aging process. But there is a lot of evidence that we may be able to retard the rate of aging. . . . Man's maximum life span is now 110 years.

Dr. Robert N. Butler, founder of the National Institute on Aging, authored the Nobel-prizewinning book, *Why Survive? Being Old in America.* He says the nation is in the midst of a geriatric revolution. During the 20th century, average life expectancy has increased from 48 to 74 years, and the number of Americans over 65 has jumped from 3 to nearly 12 percent of the population. By the time the postwar baby boom reaches retirement age, the over-65 age group will constitute one-fifth of the population. By contrast, during the American Revolution, only one-fiftieth of the population was over 65.

Other Times and Places
Literature paints a dreary picture of old age. Many of us learned in school about the seven stages of man as described by Shakespeare: "The sixth stage shifts into the lean and

slipper'd pantaloon, with spectacles on nose and pouch on side . . . his shrunk shank and . . . childish treble" voice. In the seventh stage he slips into "second childishness and mere oblivion, sans teeth, sans eyes, sans taste, sans everything (*As You Like It*, Act II, Sc. 7).

William Butler Yeats at 60 lamented: "This caricature, decrepit age that has tied to me as a dog's tail."

Even the preacher in Ecclesiastes saw old age as pretty grim. He scrutinized "man under the sun," that is, man living his natural life apart from God, and said it all added up to vanity—emptiness, disappointment, a striving after wind. He poetically described old age as the time of "evil days," when you'll say, "I have no delight in them." In old age, eyesight grows dim, arms tremble, the back stoops, teeth are few, hearing is impaired, sleep is restless, hair is white, legs are weak (Ecc. 12:1-8).

Simone de Beauvoir, the French writer, has made an exhaustive study of old age in her book, *The Coming of Age*. She says that France in the 17th century was exceedingly hard on the aged. Society was authoritarian and absolutist. The adults who ruled it allowed the children and the aged—people who did not belong to the same category as themselves—no place at all. Old age in itself commanded no respect. It was the wealthy man, the landowner, the leader, and the dignitary who was respected.

The Yaghan, a people living on the coasts of Tierra del Fuego, South America, are among the most primitive of all known tribes. They have no axes, fishhooks, cooking utensils or pots. Yet nature provides enough for the parents to be able to feed their children and have time to look after them. In their turn, the children see to it that their old parents lack for nothing.

Likewise, the Objibway Indians of North America traditionally treated everyone kindly, including their old people.

Of course, we all know about the respect for elders in traditional China and other oriental societies. When we were in Korea for our younger son's wedding, we learned about the enormous respect there for age. People politely asked us how old we were—the older the better. We learned that at 60 a father retires and lets his oldest son support him, while he "plays with the grandchildren."

Our new daughter-in-law told us that while old age was very much respected, and older sons took their responsibility seriously, girls didn't want to marry older sons. In the Orient, young people may feel oppressed by their elders, but old age is not regarded as a curse.

What Is Old?

In America, "old" has a bad sound. It carries overtones of obsolescence, breakdown, inefficiency, stylelessness. So we use marvelous evasions to keep from saying "old." We talk about "senior citizens," "golden-agers," "retired folk," or "people of mature years." We admit to being "past my prime," "no spring chicken, but not over the hill," "getting on though still kicking," "not as young as I used to be, but then who is?" But "old"? Perish the thought!

Nobody ever goes to an "old people's home." They go to "rest homes," or "nursing homes," or "retirement homes." Or to "sunset villas" or "leisure lodges" or some kind of "haven."

Yet, "old" should mean that you've lived, you've ripened, you've mellowed. You've survived some storms and stresses, you've learned to bend but not break. You may require a little more repair work to keep functioning. But an old house *can* be even more beautiful than a new one.

We make a great issue of preserving historic buildings. "Historic" means something has stood the test of time. An old person has stood the test of time.

Studies show that most older people don't feel old. They

feel themselves to be the persons they always were. If their health is good, they feel young. The fact that so many years have passed seems unreal—except for the rich memories and the lessons learned.

Seneca, the Roman philosopher, wrote in a letter to Lucilius, "We should cherish old age and enjoy it. It is full of pleasure if you know how to use it. Fruit tastes most delicious just when its season is ending." We would agree. A poet has written,

> Let me grow lovely, growing old—
> So many fine things do:
> Laces, and ivory, and gold,
> And silks need not be new;
> And there is healing in old trees,
> Old streets a glamour hold;
> Why may not I, as well as these,
> Grow lovely, growing old?
> (Karle Wilson Baker)

We haven't come across anybody yet who really wanted to be young again, to live his life all over. For the evening of life brings with it its lamp. The young can feel only young, but the old can feel both old and young at the same time. We have such a rich pool of memories and resources to dip into at will. We like the better perspective that age affords. We like the freedom, the having learned how to cope with the challenges and concerns of life. We like what the years have taught us about what matters and what doesn't.

Myths About "Old"

The negative attitude toward old age in America is actually based on a number of myths. These persist even though they fail to coincide with the facts. For example, one popular myth is that most old people end up in nursing homes. The fact is that 9 out of 10 people over 65 are able to be totally independent. Only 5 percent are in any kind of institution, and only 1 out of 5 will ever enter a nursing home even for a short time.

And of those who do enter nursing homes, half have no families. It's a myth that Americans don't take care of aging family members. One family we know cared for three aged and ailing parents in their home—his mother, her mother and father. One had heart trouble, one had suffered a debilitating stroke, one had cancer. Finally, Bill had to put his mother into a nursing home because of the kind of care she needed. He said doing so was the most traumatic experience of his whole life. He felt he had failed as a son because he and his wife could no longer carry on.

Americans do have strong feelings of family responsibility for the aged.

In contrast to his Book of Ecclesiastes, Solomon also viewed old age as the reward and crown of a good life: "Gray hair is a crown of splendor; it is attained by a righteous life" (Prov. 16:31, NIV). The climax of Job's life is that "he died, old and full of years" (Job 42:17, NIV). David, "a man after God's own heart," is described as dying "in a ripe old age, full of days, riches and honor (1 Chron. 29:28).

Abraham offers a picture of a full life. "And Abraham breathed his last and died in a ripe old age, an old man and satisfied with life; and he was gathered to his people" (Gen. 25:8).

When does old age begin? In some societies decrepitude begins at 40, in others at 80. In primitive societies, few individuals reach the age of 65—rarely as many as 3 percent. In such societies, 50 is looked upon as being old or even very old.

Dante thought old age began at 45. Victor Hugo said 40 was the old age of youth and 50 the youth of old age.

The Apostle Paul referred to himself as "Paul, the aged," at about age 60 (Philemon 9). We don't call 60 "aged."

So there's enormous difference in aging in different times and in different societies. There's evidence that a person of 65 today in our society is biologically as young as a person of 40 to 45 was in 1900.

In addition to differences in the meaning of age, there's the difference in biological aging. Nothing mysterious happens at age 65 to make a person suddenly start to fall apart.

When Bart reached age 65 it was whispered around the church that the dread event had occurred. What was *he* going to do? What were *they* going to do? They had just put up a big building. The church was growing, the debt was enormous. Who else could ever take over that responsibility? Bart had just taken on a new and capable assistant— some thought for the purpose of succeeding him. Only one person said, "When are you going to step down and give a younger person a chance?"

But Bart had built the church. In the process he had created jobs for a dozen people, including three ministers. His health and joy in his work hadn't changed. Why should he retire?

For that whole year we felt winds of uneasiness rifling the congregation. But he passed that sacred age when everyone is supposed to grow old, and nothing happened. The only problems were how to find additional parking space and what kind of addition to build. People stopped worrying about that dreaded drop-off age. Now they act as if Bart's going to last forever. He's recently had to cope with pressure to move to another location and build a still bigger church to take care of all the people. Instead, we've started a second branch—a job for still another younger minister.

As a pastor, Bart has listened to complaints about the horrors of old age from people who were much younger than he. Their tone said he knew nothing about the problems of advanced age and should be enlightened.

Compensations

Old age is not a sudden drop-off, nor even a simple slope that everyone slides down at the same rate. It's rather a succession of levels down which some move more quickly than others.

Aging is a process of compensation. Decline sets in only when you finally lose the power to make further compensations.

A girl who decides she wants to become a ballet dancer is told at 15 it's too late. She has to start at 8 or 9. Even if she attains success—with a major company in New York—she may be fired at age 28 or 35 as too old.

Billie Jean King was referred to as "the old woman of tennis" at 39. She was beaten by a girl less than half her age. A baseball player is old at 35; a swimmer may be past his prime at 24.

On the other hand, an orchestra conductor seems to improve with age. Many go on into their 80s. The pianist Arthur Rubenstein gave a brilliant concert at age 90. Pablo Casals, the cellist, continued a productive career until the end of his life at 96.

We begin to slow down at age 20. At that age the time lapse between stimulus and response starts to lengthen.

Many factors contribute to the speed of decline: health, heredity, environment, emotions, standard of living, traumatic experiences, style of life or former habits.

An executive who retires from his company at 65 doesn't suddenly lose his ability. He may go on to a new career in business or as a volunteer. Bart admits to having less animal energy than he had in his 20s, but he's more effective as a pastor than he's ever been. He's conscious of a multitude of compensations. We'll share with you specific compensations which you can make as the years go on.

When a person all at once seems to turn old, which may happen to any of us at any time, it's not that his organs suddenly lose their power. It's rather that his carefully built structure of compensations suddenly lacks the strength to hold everything together. Sometimes it's a matter of spiritual or psychological collapse—doctors call it losing "the will to live." Yet if no shock occurs, a person may go on compensating to a very advanced age with no appreciable difference in performance.

We first knew Louise Atcheson as a professional deaconness on our staff when we came to Detroit 27 years ago. She taught a large women's Bible class. She also called on the old and feeble, nurtured and nourished people, especially those in trouble. At that time she must have been 65 years old, but no one took note of the fact. She simply went right on with her work among the sick and old and needy.

Strong and active, she continued in a full-time capacity for some 20 years. Then she "retired" and moved to Livonia, and our church contributed to her support on a pension basis. She lived in her own apartment and continued to call on the sick and shut-ins. She would drive "old people" who couldn't get there themselves, to their doctor and hospital appointments, though they were years younger than she.

We were aware from the beginning that Mrs. Atcheson had raised two daughters alone. As the years went on, she suffered several heart attacks and several small strokes. At last she could no longer drive, but a retired doctor decided that driving her around to her calls would be his retirement mission in life. He was around 70 when he was driving her around at age 90. She had made one compensation after another to keep going, and still seemed the same person we had known 27 years before. When she was 91, I heard her lead a seminar on old age. I thought I would hear her discuss her own saga of struggle. But not yet. Her thoughts were still entirely on the problems and possibilities of old people, and what we can all do to help—as if she herself were not in that category at all. It seemed as if she would go on forever.

But recently word came from her at her daughter's home that she wants us to pray that the Lord will take her. She's had another slight stroke, but suddenly she's unable to make any more compensations. She's 92. We all think she has struggled valiantly and we're not ready to see her go yet. She's been a contributing member of society all these years.

Game Plans

When should you start thinking about old age? Some people talk about "the big 4-0" as the traumatic birthday. I first felt old age coming into view at age 35. Before that I occasionally joked about "old age creeping up," and people would laugh—as I expected. At 35 it hit me that I was halfway to the biblical three score years and ten. I stopped joking about "old age creeping up" because I could see it was. That was my time to think about whether my life was going to be uphill all the way, or downhill from there on. Is youth all that counts?

People consciously or unconsciously choose one of many different game plans in regard to old age. Long before you get to 65, you define your own old age by the game plan you choose.

> *If only, when one heard*
> *That Old Age was coming*
> *One could bolt the door,*
> *Answer "Not at home"*
> *And refuse to meet him!*
> (Anonymous)

"I just want to drop dead suddenly," some young folks say

pompously. Who doesn't? Youth thinks it prefers death to old age. But when the time comes, people usually prefer old age. To many people in active life, senior citizens represent a different species they can't identify with. "I'll never live to be old," they say. Their jokes about the shuffling gait, the quavering voice of old age seem to prove "old" has nothing to do with them.

■ Evade. Some seek to evade old age by living fast. "I'd rather enjoy life now than follow all the rules and live a long time." But you may live a long time anyway, and pay for past bad habits with a host of ailments.

■ Drop out. Some greet old age as a time to give up and drop out. "Let the younger people carry the responsibilities now. I've served my time." They drag out their days without ever trying to learn anything, contribute anything, or change in any way. They tell the same stories over and over again, and complain drearily about pains and worries until people stay away from them. Then the old people complain they're lonely, nobody cares. But vegetating leads to boredom, boredom makes you boring, boring people attract few companions. This game plan looks easy, but it's lethal.

■ Postpone. Still another game plan is to work hard all your life, save everything—money, time, recreation—for retirement. Then you'll enjoy a perpetual vacation—you think. You'll then have time to catch up on all the things you always wanted to do.

Several times Bart has officiated at the funeral service of someone who died of a heart attack—just when he was ready to start that all-important first retirement trip.

Did the stress of something so new cause the heart attack? Nobody knows. But it's foolish to postpone living until retirement. Another reason not to choose this game plan: When at last you have the time, you may find you have lost the taste for certain activities. Long years of neglect can kill once-healthy interests.

■ Pretend. Another game plan is to ignore old age by pretending that the life and activities of middle-age can go on and on and on. Some bring this off, especially if they're self-employed, but not many are in a position to do so.

■ Live your plans. The secret of a successful game plan is to examine your potentials, set your goals, and live your plans. An English proverb says that they who would be young when they're old must be old when they're young. That doesn't mean taking the joy out of life. It just means focusing for the long view. It means choosing those activities that add up to increasing rather than decreasing satisfaction. It means gauging yourself for the long pull—accepting the fact that life is a struggle to the end. When you stop struggling, you're dead—whether the funeral has taken place yet or not.

The Bible marks out for us a really good game plan. God pronounces as happy the man whose delight is in the law of the Lord, and on whose law he meditates day and night. "He is like a tree planted by streams of water, which yields its fruit in season and whose leaf does not wither" (Ps. 1:3, NIV). If you want fruit in old age, and all the companionship, joy, satisfaction, and appreciation that goes with fruit-bearing, choose this plan.

Early in our ministry we often wondered about Bart's career, what steps to take, whom to look to for opportunities and advancement. The only plans we made for old age were that we wanted to continue ministering and teaching—in some little place, wherever needed. These verses shaped our lives: "Trust in the Lord with all your heart and lean not on your own understanding; in all your ways acknowledge Him, and He will make your paths straight" (Prov. 3:5-6, NIV).

We can't know what life holds for us. But we can choose God's plan for our lives. Whatever that is, it will work out to be right for us.

TWO ❦ GOALS– *What Are Yours?*

Age is not all decay; it is the ripening, the swelling,
of the fresh life within, that withers and bursts the husk.

George MacDonald, *The Marquis of Lossie*

As I write this chapter, Bart and I are in a cabin in the mountains. We had an extremely strenuous year, which included two trips abroad besides many smaller trips. Then we took an exciting two-week trip to Alaska, just for the adventure of it. After Alaska, we had a frantically hurried week at home catching up on church responsibilities, friends, family, and the machinery of living.

Then we landed here, and suddenly all the fast motion stopped. I'd made the reservation months ago. When I saw the place, a simple little cabin in the woods, I thought, "How can I possibly spend three whole weeks here—away from the comforts and luxuries of home? No radio, no TV,

19

no telephone, no entertainment of any kind except a swimming pool nearby. Not even any good restaurants near enough to get to very often."

Now, a week later, we love it. We walk, we swim, we study, we read. The time is going all too fast. Bart is outlining his sermons for the whole year. He's up to March already. I finished writing my next year's Bible course and now have a beautiful opportunity to work on this book. The only sounds we hear are the birds, the squirrels, the bubbling stream at our back door. The occasional hum of a passing car is just enough sound to keep us children of civilization from feeling too far off in the wilderness.

These three weeks are a time of stringently facing the resources within us to entertain ourselves. It's a time of self-discipline, of keeping to a schedule, of getting things done, of relaxing. We're feeling the tempo of the quiet lives of the people who live in this area. But without goals, I couldn't have faced it, even for three weeks.

Debunking the Myths

It is a myth that old people can't learn, can't change or grow. It's a myth that old people become increasingly rigid, bound to the past, that they can't move forward. They don't all live in the past, behind the times, aimless and wandering in mind.

The fact is that 80-year-olds compete well with high school students on IQ tests, though they perform best if not limited in time. They're more deliberate, may require a little longer, but stack up well.

We see solid evidence of these facts in people we know, also in great figures of history. Some have accomplished their greatest feats after age 65. At 70, Benjamin Franklin helped write the Declaration of Independence. Frank Lloyd Wright created some of his best architectural works while in his 80s. He completed New York's spiraling Guggenheim

Museum when he was 91. Douglas MacArthur became commander of the United Nations Forces in Korea at age 70. He led the troops in battle until President Truman fired him. After saying, "Old soldiers never die, they just fade away," he became a successful businessman.

President Reagan celebrated his 70th birthday shortly after becoming President, and has now announced for a second term. No one suggests that his age interferes with his discharge of duties.

For the great majority of older people, mental ability stays the same or even improves. Compensations in judgment or skill can make up for slight loss of certain kinds of memory.

But what about emotional problems? Some psychiatrists are discovering that older people may suffer from depressions, neuroses, schizophrenia, the same as people of any age. But these illnesses are not necessarily part of old age.

What is often called "senility" may in fact be rooted in a physical condition. It may be due to reversible disorders such as hypoglycemia or anemia. Or it may be due to Alzheimer's disease, where the brain deteriorates. But even that is a disease. It can strike as early as 40, and is not inherent in old age itself.

So with the old myths of failing intellect out of the way, we can get on with taking charge of our lives. Dr. Paul Parker, a family physician practicing in Glen Ellyn, Illinois, asks his patients past 65 to set goals for themselves as if they were going to live to be 100. With all I've been reading about the lengthening of life through diet and medical treatments, I've been revising my plans. I'd previously set my sights on living about as long as my parents. They died at ages 72 and 74—as I thought, "old and full of years." Those ages are looking younger all the time, and my health is way better than theirs was.

"The world is so full of a number of things, I'm sure we

should all be as happy as kings," said Robert Louis Stevenson in his *Child's Garden of Verses*. I've loved that little
poem since childhood. Certainly there are enough good
things in life to keep us happy and occupied all our lives.
But we have to get out into the fields where the flowers
grow to find the good things for ourselves. If we aim only at
manipulating other people into bringing bouquets to us,
we're doomed for disappointment.

Deceptive Goals
Literature and life are full of people who chose deceptive
goals. Shakespeare's *Macbeth* immortalizes the person who
ruins his life by ambition. After Macbeth got what he
wanted—the kingship—by murdering the king, he said,

> *I have lived long enough; my way of life*
> *Is fall'n into the sear, the yellow leaf;*
> *And that which should accompany old age,*
> *As honour, love, obedience, troops of friends,*
> *I must not look to have; but in their stead,*
> *Curses, not loud but deep; mouth-honour, breath,*
> *Which the poor heart would fain deny, and dare not.*
> (Act V, Sc. 3)

A little later, Macbeth called life "a tale told by an idiot,
full of sound and fury, signifying nothing" (Act V, Sc. 5).

In Arthur Miller's play, *Death of a Salesman*, we feel the
tragedy of the little man who simply chose the wrong goals
in life. He rejected following his true gift, carpentry, to
become a traveling salesman. He thought that offered more
money and an easier life. He put his values on being well
liked, on the big bluff, the fast line, the lie, the right contacts, the outward impression. His life collapsed when his
values couldn't carry him into the later years of life.

The play must have struck a responsive chord in many

different cultures. Since 1949, it has been performed in every major city of the world, including Peking. In addition, it has been read by over two million people.

However, even setting great goals and reaching them isn't a cure-all in itself. Ernest Hemingway was told by a teacher that he could never become a writer, that he didn't have the right style. He lived to win a Nobel prize for literature, to influence the writing style of a whole generation. But in the end he committed suicide. Failing health made him feel he could no longer write. Furthermore, he couldn't continue to project to the world an image of the great sportsman, overflowing with vitality and manliness.

Jeremiah tells us how to deal with goals that can become deceptive:

> Let not a wise man boast of his wisdom,
> and let not the mighty man boast of his might,
> let not a rich man boast of his riches;
> but let him who boasts boast of this,
> that he understands and knows Me,
> that I am the Lord (Jer. 9:23-24).

Spiritual Goals

Elizabeth Holmes, a retired school principal, says that one of her primary goals is a deepening knowledge of the Bible. "I want to be able to see below the surface, to get deep insights for myself." She's an effective and greatly respected Christian leader, an advisor in Christian education. But she wants more understanding of God's Word. That's her long-term aim. And to implement it, she attends Bible classes, reads commentaries, takes Bible courses. She spends time every day reading and pondering the Bible. She doesn't feel she has arrived just because she is accepted as a Christian leader. Her personal goal, she says, is to be like the 17th-century monk, Brother Lawrence—every moment experiencing the presence of God.

The Bible has a lot to say about how the fear of God, or the knowledge of God, prolongs life. (See Proverbs 3:1-2, 13, 16; 9:11-12; 10:27; 16:31.) It says that true wisdom starts with the fear of the Lord—awe, respect, worshipful attitude toward Him. We're to dig for wisdom as for hidden treasure—because we'll find great reward in wisdom.

To select the right goals, we have to fight fragmentation. When we find our true selves, we find that we're needed, that there's a niche in society for us, that we're appreciated. God has created just about the percentage of musicians, artists, preachers, bookkeepers, administrators, teachers, healers, helpers that society needs. There are a lot more teachers and helpers than brilliant musicians because more are needed.

If we spend time alone with God, alone with the Bible, we absorb His sense of values. We find ourselves. We find what we in our deepest hearts really want to be and do. We find what God wants us to do. Shakespeare said it in a worldly context:

> This above all: to thine own self be true,
> And it must follow, as the night the day,
> Thou canst not then be false to any man.
> (Hamlet, Act 1, Sc. 3)

The Bible says it over and over again when it shows great figures going off into the wilderness. They went to be alone with God to find themselves, to find their mission. Old age often offers the gift of silence, of time to be alone, to invite God. But long before we get to old age, we have to find little oases of silence in our daily lives. If we keep on trying to meet all the demands of job, children, grandchildren, church, friends, community we'll fly into a thousand pieces and lose all sense of personal integrity.

Jesus said, "If you abide in My Word, then you are truly disciples of Mine; and you shall know the truth, and the truth shall make you free" (John 8:31-32). The freedom of life in Christ is wonderful. You can give up feeling pressured, you can resist letting the world press you into its mold. You don't even have to let church people press you into a mold.

Remember when Elijah was rebellious and discouraged? He found his peace with God in the desert at Mount Horeb. Remember how John the Baptist spent his days in silence in the desert until the day of his public appearance? On the quiet Island of Patmos God gave the Apostle John his visions. Jesus repeatedly went out into the wilderness to pray. Even He needed quiet and meditation.

Paul spent three years in the desert of Arabia, between his conversion and his first public appearance. From that time on he never seemed to have had the slightest doubt about his goal in life:

> "I want to know Christ and the power of His resurrection and the fellowship of sharing in His sufferings, becoming like Him in His death . . . Not that I have already obtained all this . . . But one thing I do: Forgetting what is behind and straining toward what is ahead, I press on toward the goal to win the prize for which God has called me heavenward in Christ Jesus" (Phil. 3:10-14, NIV).

Bible teaching has given me the structure I need to escape the emptiness of an overly busy life. I can resist the pressures in order to prepare that next lesson. My necessary study time includes time to think and dream and pray and meditate, time for my soul to catch up with my body, time to listen to God speaking to me. If I miss one day, I'll more than catch up another. I can say I *have* to do it—I have a class to teach.

You must figure out the structure or discipline it takes to give your life the focus it needs.

Man is incurably spiritual. Many have tried to take the Bible away from him by picking holes in it. But without the Bible, people only find something else to believe in—spiritism, astrology, Satanism, or any one of the dozens of new sects that have sprung up.

We all have many competing selves. We must set priorities. To become like Christ is a wonderful and comprehensive goal in life. Like Him in our close relationship with God. Like Him in our balance between activity and quietness. Like Him in the depth of our relationships. Like Him in the joy of meeting people's needs.

I personally think that meeting needs is the way to find happiness in life. If you insist on singing solos when nobody wants to listen to you, you're doomed for heartache and disappointment. If you long to be president when you're marvelously appreciated as a helper, you're courting disappointment. *If you're willing to do the thing you're most appreciated for doing, you increase, you grow, you develop, and others are blessed in the process.*

As the years go on, it becomes increasingly important—and possible—to be ourselves, seeking God's leading as to the goals we should set for ourselves. Success is knowing not only your abilities but also your limitations. "Do not think of yourself more highly than you ought, but rather think of yourself with sober judgment, in accordance with the measure of faith God has given you" (Rom. 12:3, NIV).

Lifestyle Goals

Says Dr. Paul Parker, "The problem I meet over and over again in my practice is the lifestyle of my patients. Older people come in complaining of all kinds of ailments, thinking these are inevitable as the years pile up, wanting me to give them some magic pill that will make everything go away. They have brought so many of these ailments on themselves by their way of living. They're overfed and underexercised. Along with telling them they should make their plans as if they're going to live to be 100, I set before them three important goals that will open up new worlds for anybody:

■ Become physically fit through diet and exercise.

■ Get involved with children—to meet their needs, and to enjoy seeing the world through their eyes.

■ Set up a plan for regular, intercessory prayer. Pray for missionaries all over the world. Get involved with someone in need. You'll find yourself moved to help meet those needs."

These three goals, he says, will keep anybody busy until the age of 100 and beyond.

Many people have major projects, a piece of art, something related to homemaking, home building projects, or gardening. You can read, study, take courses, learn from others in these areas. Dr. Carroll Munshaw, former professor of education, says when he retired he had 38 or more projects he wanted to do around his house and yard. He wanted to plant a new flower garden, put in shelves, do remodeling, repairing. Each day he has several projects lined up.

Harriet Beecher Stowe said, "In all ranks of life the human heart yearns for the beautiful; and the beautiful things that God makes are His gift to all alike." You can grow beautiful things. You can make beautiful things with your hands. These are appropriate expressions for one created in God's image. "He has made everything beautiful in its time" (Ecc. 3:11, NIV). God Himself obviously loves beauty.

Others make a project of finances. After my father died, my mother, to my amazement, began reading the financial news, followed her stocks closely, learned to make good investments. She also had a large garden which she greatly enjoyed supervising. She canned, froze, stored up quantities of food for the winter—for herself and her visiting children. Cutting down expenses to match income can be a great game.

Elizabeth Holmes enjoyed economizing as a game. "When I was bringing up my children alone, providing a medical education for my son on a school principal's salary, I considered money a challenge. I had a fight on my hands. I had to win over that money. There's always been something challenging to me about making do."

Relationship Goals

You'll also need goals for your relationships, if you're going to have relationships. You can squash them all as you move along through the years. Or you can plant and cultivate a veritable garden of good relationships.

What relationships do you want to carry with you through the years? What new ones do you want to create? What do you want at the end? Whatever your answers, you need to set positive goals for learning to listen, support, help, meet needs, and keep in touch in order to maintain or build relationships.

Someone has said hardening of the heart ages people more quickly than hardening of the arteries. To resist the rigidity of old age, we must combine the efforts of body, mind, and heart. That means exercising for the body, studying for the mind, and loving for the heart.

Gerontologists say factors that contribute to the problems of older people are social ostracism, a shrinking circle of friends, loneliness, reduction and loss of self-respect, feelings of self-disgust.

But these are problems we all have to deal with ourselves. We can't gain attention, respect, or friends by demanding. We have to earn these things when we're old, as well as at any other age, or they're not real. There's no satisfaction in phony relationships, phony respect, or attention that springs only from a sense of duty.

Goals and Your Gifts

A few weeks ago Bill Vande Kieft, who attends our church, called up and asked, "Do you like fish? I can bring you some fresh fish that I caught." I assured him we'd love to have some. When he brought over a plate of fish, I realized he'd be a good person to talk to about goals.

"Goals?" He came in and sat down. "One of my goals is to be the best fisherman on the lake. I guess I am that already. To be a good fisherman I use all the helps I can get. I wouldn't dream of fishing without a depth sounder. I ascertain the depths of the lake all over, then calculate by the weather and the seasons what the temperature of the water would be at certain depths and in certain places. Then I fish in those places.

"And I make a study of baits. I make my own lures— flashing things that look to the fish like a school of minnows maybe. The best bait is live worms. So I have to make a study of where and when I can find the best worms. They have to be alive and wiggling to be good bait.

"Work? I can take it or leave it. I always enjoyed my work as an executive in a car company. But when offered early retirement, I took it. That was four years ago. I've always had so many projects going that it is no problem to me to be retired. I keep up my home, do all the repairs myself. I also have a hobby of shortwave radio. My goal in that is to be able to pull in every part of the world. I can now, but there's always more to learn, little refinements to make in my equipment. One day I pull in South Africa, another day I may get Australia, or Alaska. Last week I picked up a missionary in Nigeria trying to get through to Michigan to place an order for hospital supplies. I picked up his message and managed to relay it. I felt pretty good about that.

"I've always had so much to do in retirement, I don't know how I found time to go to work. But I'm not satisfied with my life yet. I want to be giving a bigger hunk of my time to the Lord."

The later years, after the children are grown, can be a glorious time for discovering a whole new level of living. You're free from so much responsibility and you have time. Grandma Moses discovered she had a talent for painting only after she became too old to do manual labor.

To discover your own abilities, study the chapters in the Bible on gifts—Romans 12, 1 Corinthians 12, Ephesians 4, 1 Peter 4. Take aptitude tests and courses. Try a lot of new things, ask other people what they think you're good at. Or spend time developing a talent you know you have had all along but didn't have time to pursue.

It may prove a great satisfaction to give up at last all high-flying "oughts" and settle down to be comfortable with what you really are. In his Journal entry for July 14, 1852, Thoreau wrote: "The youth gets together his materials to build a bridge to the moon, or perchance a palace or temple on the earth, and at length the middle-aged man concludes to build a woodshed with them." Bart and I have always thought that sounded sad, but maybe it's really quite a happy thought. How nice at last to come to terms with yourself. How satisfying to use all your abilities to do well what you are thoroughly equipped to do.

Making It Happen

The most marvelous goals in the world won't give you any satisfaction if you don't make progress toward realizing them. Peter Marshall said, "Small deeds done are better than great deeds planned." There are definite steps in achieving a goal.

■ Be as specific as possible, so that you can be aware each day of having taken at least one little step toward that goal.

■ Break up your distant goal into little steps you can manage one at a time. The management books call these steps objectives.

Sometimes, for example, I set a goal of housecleaning. I resolve to clean and get rid of every speck of excess in the garage, basement, shelves, drawers, boxes. I couldn't face all this at once. I couldn't face three weeks at it, the way my mother used to do every spring at housecleaning time. But I can face one drawer each day, and somedays even pick up speed and do considerably more than one. Nobody really knows that housecleaning is going on, not even Bart. But I can go to bed knowing I have accomplished my little objective for that day, along with my regular responsibilities.

Bart does the same thing in his church work. When we go to a new place, we have a picture in our minds. The Lord has shown us what He wants to accomplish through us in that particular ministry. You don't build a church out of nothing all at once. You build a church—or anything else—brick by brick. Bart divides his seemingly impossible dream into the tiny little steps he needs to take each day. It always amazes me that he knows the next little step to take. Then he takes it. He's not content to end a single day without in some way working toward his goal.

When you divide a big project into tiny steps compatible with your nature and temperament, the project becomes fun—a joyous experience. You don't beat yourself for not accomplishing the whole thing all at once. You have many little celebrations and satisfactions along the way. And you feel forever young in the process.

THREE ❦ HABITS— Help or Hindrance?

For the ordinary business of life,
an ounce of habit is worth a pound of intellect.

Thomas B. Reed

Habit can be a wonderful ladder of support enabling us to attain what is otherwise out of reach. Or habit can be like the pillory, holding us in a rigid position that cripples us.

Those who have lost the capacity to change their habits are old at 20. Those who retain the capacity to change and improve their habits seem young at 80.

Habits make it possible for us to function in life. We do a lot of things automatically. Departure from habit introduces stress.

However, none of us needs to be frozen into our particular mixture of good and bad habits.

The Bible doesn't indicate that patterns of behavior are set once we reach adulthood. It says on almost every page that we can change. "Therefore if any man is in Christ, he is a new creature; the old things passed away; behold, new things have come" (2 Cor. 5:17). Many people come to a dramatic turnaround when they find Christ as a new center for their lives. That changed central core can result in new habits spiritually, physically, emotionally, intellectually, and socially.

Even those seemingly paralyzed by bad habits can be like the paralytic brought to Jesus. For Jesus says to each of us, "Take courage, My son, your sins are forgiven" (Matt. 9:2). Christ can give the power to get up and walk—to adopt new habits.

However, we need to be careful to distinguish between what can be changed and what cannot. For centuries, the Chinese bound the feet of upper-class girls as a symbol of status. But the poor girls were crippled for life. We can cripple our children, our mates, or ourselves by trying to restrict something that is essential to personality.

Be Open to Change
However, there are many habit patterns that have nothing to do with basic personality. Some of these are as crippling as bound feet. Dr. Robert Butler, expert on aging, says ability to change and adapt actually has less to do with age than it does with lifelong character. Most people change and remain open to change throughout life. The old notion that character is laid down in final form by the fifth year of life can be confidently refuted. To live is to change.

Scientific studies of healthy older people show that they can and do change. We see older people successfully adjusting to the need for changed habits. Many alter their diet radically after a heart attack or a diagnosis of diabetes or high blood pressure.

The sooner in life we pitch out the bad habits and strengthen the good ones, the better prepared we are for the later years. Furthermore, we get many more years out of the good habits. Yet it's never too late.

Habits produce stability. When the boat rocks in a storm, we need the habit of hanging on. Even habits that are not good must be hung onto until they can be replaced bit by bit. A head psychiatrist at a veterans hospital said, "In general, we have to just try to patch up what's there and get people functioning again. Some personalities we don't dare take apart because we might not be able to put them back together again."

However, if we're willing, God can take us apart and put us back together again—whole. "Old things are passed away, all things are become new" (2 Cor. 5:17, kjv). If we've already turned our lives over to Him, we can ask Him to help us get the kinks out—one by one.

We can get excellent advice from loved ones and friends about what needs changing in us, especially if we don't see it ourselves. The writer of Proverbs said, "Faithful are the wounds of a friend" (27:6).

> *"Trust not yourself; but your defects to know,*
> *Make use of ev'ry friend—and ev'ry foe"*
> (Alexander Pope,
> "Essay on Criticism," part 2, 1.13)

Malcom Cowley, a retired writer of 80, says the three bad habits of old age are:

■ Untidiness. Old people tend to let junk pile up. Clinging to useless possessions, they get slovenly.

■ Vanity. Old people love to be praised, and seek it out. They want to hear over and over again about the great things they did in the past.

■ Greed. Old people tend to squirrel away money and are jealous of their possessions, as if they were going to live forever. He says these tendencies have to be resisted. ("The

View from 80," *Life* magazine).

Benjamin Franklin said, "Each year, one vicious habit rooted out, in time ought to make the worst man good." A nice idea. But only Christ can give us the motive power to really work on ourselves.

Mark Twain conceded the power of habit: "Habit is habit and not to be flung out of the window by any man, but coaxed downstairs a step at a time."

Sometimes the easiest way to change a habit is to throw it out all at once—as with smoking, or drinking for an alcoholic. Other times, bit by bit works best. Bart and I have totally changed our habits of eating in the last 30 years. We moved step by step into a more nutritious diet, as each of us could take it emotionally. Many people can't stand any change at all in their eating habits. To them, food is apparently more important than health.

We cannot change anyone's habits by imposing pressure from the outside. We each have to make up our own mind when and how much we want to change in any area. Habits good or bad start so insidiously. A thought or desire leads to an act, good or bad. The first time we do something it may seem difficult. The second time it's easier, the third time still easier. Soon the act leads to the habit. The composite of habit adds up to character. It's a law of life.

We need to be constantly evaluating our structure of habits as a whole, and our individual habits one by one. Changing one little habit for the better can be very satisfying. We can constantly be developing good habits that make life easier or more interesting and exciting. The structure of good habits becomes a great prop in old age.

Physical Habits
Seneca, the Roman philosopher said, "Man does not die, he kills himself." Too many of us go through life in headlong heedlessness of our bodies. They spring back so quickly

in youth that we think all we have to do is go to the doctor when something goes wrong, and he can make us well. So we get the idea that it's the doctor's job to keep our bodies well, just as it's the mechanic's job to keep our cars going.

Bart and I learned the hard way that we can't depend too much on the mechanic for our car. Before leaving for our vacation, Bart took his car in for a general checkup. He gave the instruction, "Put it in shape to travel. Do everything that needs doing." The mechanic did—or thought he did. It all cost a few hundred dollars, including four new tires.

The only thing he overlooked was putting in oil. We drove 700 miles or so, feeling secure that the car was in good shape. By the time we could get to a garage, after the heat meter came on, the engine was burned out. You can imagine what that involved. What have we learned? We're going to stop depending on a mechanic to take care of our cars and take more responsibility ourselves.

A doctor can give us medicines which we hope will make us well. We certainly need doctors for many ailments. An eye doctor, whose patient complained about the high fee for surgery, told him, "Well, why don't you just try doing it yourself then—or get a friend to do it for you?"

But when you go in for a cold, even the best doctor may forget to tell you basic truths about health. He probably won't tell you to change your lifestyle in order to prevent heart surgery later on. Or learn how to handle your stress better and improve your chances of avoiding arthritis.

Remember, good habits are just as hard to break as bad habits. Neighbors say to us, "You people are so self-disciplined. You go to that pool every day and swim your laps for a half an hour, then get out." Or in the winter, "You take those walks every day no matter what the weather. I could never get out in weather like that. How can you be so self-disciplined?"

Strangely, it doesn't feel like discipline to us. Those walks and swims feel like little oases of relaxation in the day's activities. It's just something we do, like eating breakfast, lunch, and supper, or going to bed at about the same time. We don't debate those matters each time. We do them as matter-of-factly as we put on our clothes in the morning.

Walking didn't seem easy when I started walking a mile each way to high school. But after I'd done that for four years, when I got to college and lived on campus, I didn't feel as good if I didn't walk. So I walked every day from five to six o'clock, sometimes meeting my brother to walk and enjoy a chat with him.

When Bart and I dated, he didn't have a car. Some dates were just walking, then having refreshments. So after we were married, it seemed natural to walk together. We didn't feel as good if we didn't walk. When we could, we walked together. When necessary, one of us stayed with the children while the other walked.

Even on the busiest day Bart will dash home from the church for an hour or so to walk or swim. He says he gets so tense he can't stand himself if he misses his exercise. We know we have to exercise if we want to sleep well. Studies have shown that a 15-minute walk will lower the blood pressure more than a drug.

We've never attempted jogging, because it looks like such hard work we're afraid we'd never keep it up. Walking and swimming we know we'll do because they are so enjoyable.

"Use it or lose it" is a basic law of life that applies most obviously to physical abilities. You don't have to resign yourself to losing physical strength by any certain age. I now can walk as far and swim much farther than I could in my youth. I can't say that every single day we're just dying to get over to that pool and swim. If it's a little chilly, or there are a few drops of rain in the air, we may be the only ones in the pool. But habit gets us there. We know we'll feel so much better for the next 24 hours if we just bestir ourselves and go. Habit propels us forward against the natural forces of inertia in our makeup.

Good habits of eating are acquired the same way. You feel so much better when you eat right that soon you won't eat any other way. You don't want to pay the price.

All kinds of insignificant little habits make the machinery of life run more smoothly. After losing one glove a few times, I formed the habit of carrying gloves with a finger between them. I never again lost one glove. After a few frantic searchings for my watch, I formed the habit of never laying it down at home except in a certain little drawer. Away from home, I never lay it down except in my purse. Any number of times in travel I've thought, "I forgot my watch. I wonder what I did with it. I don't have the slightest recollection of handling it at all." I look in my purse— and there it is. Habit propels me into familiar motions which aren't registering in my awareness. I keep learning improved little habits in cooking, housekeeping, and gardening. Each improvement makes life easier or pleasanter, or compensates for decreasing energy.

Douglas MacArthur said, "Live every day of your life as though you expected to live forever." Don't ever say or feel, "It's too late. There's no use changing my habits now." You can always improve your health, your efficiency, your pleasure in living. You can reduce irritations by changing your habits. To form new habits quickly, simply start and don't allow *any* exceptions. Before you know it, you'll be performing a desirable habit without thinking about it.

Spiritual Habits
Daniel was known among the administrators and satraps of Medo-Persia for his habit of regular prayer.

Now when Daniel learned that the decree had been
published, he went home to his upstairs room . . . .
Three times a day he got down on his knees and
prayed, giving thanks to his God, just as he had done
before (Dan. 6:10, NIV).

Habit carried him through a time of crisis and pressure.
Our habits of prayer and Bible reading can carry us through
also. In times when others might think of suicide, alcohol,
drugs, or dropping out as solutions, we find ourselves turning automatically to God. It's a habit—one that has to be
deliberately cultivated in the good times so that it will be in
place for the bad times.

I've seen many people who, when their worlds were col-
lapsing, were brought through spiritually by their habits.
I've seen them put one foot in front of the other through
divorce, bereavement, tragedy with children, loss of jobs.
I've seen them continue coming to church and Bible
classes, keep on praying, trusting, smiling. Habit is a wonderful support spiritually. But you need regular habits so
that you'll go to church the very next Sunday after your
loved one dies, or after your job folds up. It won't be any
easier a few weeks later—only harder.

Even Jesus had a regular habit of gathering with others
for worship. "He went to Nazareth, where He had been
brought up, and on the Sabbath Day He went into the
synagogue, as was His custom" (Luke 4:16, NIV). He didn't
say, "I won't go because the synagogue isn't perfect, it
doesn't preach what I want to hear, I don't like the way
people there look at Me." He went to worship God and to
share a life-giving message that God had given to Him.

Intellectual Habits

What are your intellectual habits? Are you open to new
ideas? Do you read magazines and books, attend classes, or

listen to serious speakers? Remember, use it or lose it. The brain isn't a muscle, but there's something up there that benefits from exercise.

We know that physically it is good to take every opportunity to move about. Bart doesn't always use the interoffice phone on his desk. He likes to jump up and run to see someone in another office. He doesn't summon others to come to him. I often wash clothes while I'm at work in my upstairs study. That means a trip down and up two flights of stairs every half hour. We used to hear that doctors wanted heart patients to have houses all on one floor. Now they tell them to exercise—develop those auxiliary blood vessels. Use it or lose it.

The same principle applies to mental exercise. A nurse said, "It's my observation that old people who have used their minds tend to keep their sharpness of mind to the end. It's those who have given up using their minds who deteriorate most markedly."

Autopsies have shown that mental alertness does not correspond with degree of hardening of the arteries of the brain. Some whose brains appeared to be seriously affected had in life been bright and alert to the very end.

Learning in old age may be affected by loss of sight or hearing, slowing of responses, worry about learning ability, lack of interest, lack of desire, or by disease. But learning itself does not decline. If the brain is used, persons may continue to learn, perhaps as well as they did at any age, perhaps better.

The Greek philosopher Solon said, "I grow old ever learning many things." Michelangelo's motto was, "I am still learning."

Samuel Johnson, the English writer, said, "It is a man's own fault, it is from want of use, if his mind grows torpid in old age" (James Boswell, *Life of Johnson*, 1778).

And the Bible says, "For whoever has, to him shall more

be given, and he shall have an abundance; but whoever does not have, even what he has shall be taken away from him" (Matt. 13:12). If you go into old age with a good structure of intellectual habits, you'll build upon and refine that structure every day of your life. If you quit reading and learning when you left school, you're already close to being dead intellectually.

What are some good intellectual habits?

■ Be conscious of your ignorance. This is the first step toward knowledge. That's the main thing an education does for you anyway. It opens your eyes to how much you don't know.

■ Learn from experience. We learned a costly lesson from not checking our oil ourselves. It took us all these years for our habits of totally depending on others to catch up with us. We vow we won't have to learn the same lesson again. This is learning the hard way.

■ Learn from what you're told. We should have read those car manuals more carefully. That would be learning the easy way. Some of the "plain country folk," as they call themselves, who live in the mountains near our vacation cabin, were absolutely horrified that we could be so stupid as to let our automobile's oil go down.

■ Build on what you already know. Said Seneca, "An old man learning his ABCs is a disgraceful and absurd object; the young man must store up, the old man must use" (*Epistulae ad Lucilium*, Epis. xxxvi, 4). It would be foolish for Bart to start out now to become an expert mechanic. To remember to keep enough oil in his car is a more modest and attainable goal. But I told him recently, "You are only now beginning to realize your full potential as a speaker. You've always been so busy building a church that you couldn't give the time to speaking that you can now." He's building on what he already can do.

■ Keep learning. "The larger the island of knowledge, the

longer the shoreline of wonder" (Ralph W. Sockman).

You can add to your knowledge of God by studying. You can learn something new about Him every day of your life and never plumb the depths of all there is to learn from the Bible. "Be diligent to present yourself approved to God as a workman who does not need to be ashamed, handling accurately the Word of truth" (2 Tim. 2:15). Set out to understand the Bible as a whole.

■ Stay flexible. Hardening of the ideas can bring on old age faster than hardening of the arteries. We need to keep flexible, keep adaptable, keep open to new ideas.

Most Americans value education as a business asset, as a tool. But the years from middle age on are a time to learn to appreciate education as an experience. Middle age, like adolescence, has been noted as a time of upheaval, of dissatisfaction, of restlessness, of reevaluation. Both can presage a future period of growth. In middle age you begin to think about what you've missed. And you can begin to discover anew the joy of learning, of intellectual experience. You can share what the great minds of the past and present have to offer. You can stretch your mind to encompass things you thought you'd never understand.

Old age can be a time for broadening horizons, setting ourselves free from earlier prejudices.

■ Appreciate new experiences. Seek to get acquainted with people who differ from you in background or viewpoint. We love to travel back to places we first saw decades ago. The original freshness isn't there, but there's delight in reinforcing old impressions, correcting false impressions, seeing what we missed before.

And when we go to a totally new place—like China, or Alaska—we feel young again, with a whole new world opening to our imagination.

■ Don't lose your intellectual appetite. Keep hold of a motive—for us it's ever looking for new ideas or illustrations for teaching or speaking. For others the motive is personal satisfaction, or showing pictures of trips, or enriched conversation. Constant learning means you're able to talk to those in the thick of life. You're keeping up even through the rapids of change in our society. It takes knowledge and skill to maneuver the rapids.

The habit of always learning keeps you from narrowing your field of interest to yourself—your temperature, your pulse, your digestion, your feelings, your pains. You are better off if you don't live in your own world exclusively.

Age seems to have little to do with intellectual accomplishment. McCormick was 23 when he invented the reaper, but Verdi wrote an opera at age 80. Westinghouse was only 23 when he invented the air brake, but Goethe finished writing *Faust* at 80. Thomas Jefferson wrote the Declaration of Independence at 33, but Justice Oliver Wendell Holmes was still writing brilliant opinions at 90.

Lifelong habits of mind seem to be a more determining factor in intellectual accomplishment than age. Whatever your age, it's a good time to shore up those habits of mind. Hold onto your own independent tastes and judgment. Resist being drawn into the vortex of mindless conformity with the popular taste.

Emotional and Social Habits

How we behave is as much a matter of habit as of inborn temperament. Overcoming bad emotional habits is possible at any age. "He who is slow to anger is better than the mighty, and he who rules his spirit, than he who captures a city" (Prov. 16:32). We're to cultivate habits of emotion that make us healthy, at peace with ourselves, open to relationships with family and friends. We're to develop self-control. God wouldn't have commanded us to love if it weren't possible for us to change our attitudes.

In old age, you can either shut yourself up, claiming

nobody understands you, or you can open up and try to understand others. It is important to form habits of relating to other people in church activities, community efforts, and of meeting needs of neighbors. You dare not spend all your time working, supposing that when you retire you'll make friends. Cultivating people is as much a habit as walking or studying. You need to keep your social skills honed by use.

One way to perfect your social skills is to become part of a home Bible study. Study with others what the Bible has to say about developing relationships.

How can you form all these wonderful new habits? John Ruskin, the great educator, said:

> The entire object of true education is to make people not merely to do the right things, but enjoy them; not merely industrious, but to love industry; not merely learned, but to love knowledge; not merely pure, but to love purity; not merely just, but to hunger and thirst after justice.

FOUR ❧
WORK—
Who Needs It?

Thank God every morning when you get up that you have something to do that day which must be done whether you like it or not.

Charles Kingsley,
Town and Country Sermons

Throughout our lives we have had instilled within us the idea that work is desirable—until 65, that is. Approximately the first 25 years of life are preparation. During this time a person receives much support in education, training, expectations. Family, schools, bosses teach him that he must work and he'd better learn to like it. If possible, love it.

From ages 25 to 45 a person experiences his growth years as an employee—though many professional people go on to far greater achievements after age 45. Around 45 he becomes aware of the limits of his abilities. He starts trying to conserve what he has achieved. He feels a slight decrease in some physical abilities and energies, but feels continued pressure for achievement. In the middle adult years, demands and expectations often exceed abilities and energies. This group may be carrying both old and young on its back, and often feels overburdened.

At age 65, a person may still feel he is at the very peak of his abilities. And suddenly nothing is expected. Work evaporates. He experiences a terrible gap between his own capacities and society's expectations. All too many capable individuals are suddenly turned out to pasture at 65 with the traditional gold watch and a speech.

Importance of Work

An enormous amount is written today about all the things we should be doing *for* old people—as if they were incompetents. This is one of the myths. Remember, only one-tenth of those over 65 are unable to live independently. Each of us needs to think in terms of working, of contributing in some way to the end of our days. We have a shocking amount of life still ahead of us at age 65. For women it's an average of 18 years, for men it's 14 years. That's too long to sit and watch.

Diogenes, the Greek philosopher, was told that he should take a rest because he was an old man. He replied, "If I were running in the stadium, ought I to slacken my pace when approaching the goal? Ought I not rather to put on speed?"

Longfellow, 19th-century American poet, believed we should be:

> Up and doing,
>   With a heart for any fate;
> Still achieving, still pursuing,
>   Learn to labor and to wait.

God provided us with work from the day we first arrived on this planet. "Then the Lord God took the man and put him into the Garden of Eden to cultivate it and keep it" (Gen. 2:15). That work was pleasant and creative. But man disobeyed in the one simple test of obedience he was given. After he had chosen not to be in complete harmony with God, he needed toil. "By the sweat of your face you shall eat bread, till you return to the ground" (Gen. 3:19). There would be thorns and thistles to plague him. Woman would be bound up in this struggle through her desire for her husband.

I don't notice anything here about retirement. It sounds like we're to work to the end.

The fourth commandment asks us not to work on the Sabbath Day. It also commands us to labor for six days. "Six days you shall labor and do all your work" (Ex. 20:9). I don't notice any age limits here—that you work till age 65, then turn to jelly while everyone else carries the load. Work is for yourself, to keep you comfortable, safe, belonging, esteemed.

The Book of Proverbs has a great deal to say about work. We're to take a pattern from the ants. "Go to the ant, O sluggard . . ." (Prov. 6:6-11). Ants work in cooperation with each other; they work diligently; they work around obstacles, they appear undiscourageable. The sluggard, on the other hand, lets the weeds grow, lets his walls fall down just by indulging in "a little sleep, a little slumber, a little folding of the hands to rest" (Prov. 24:30-34). He makes an excuse of anything, moves only in the same spot without going forward, and refuses criticism (Prov. 26:13-16).

Jesus glorified simple toil by working in the carpenter's shop. He also glorified the labor of teaching and healing.

Paul said simply, "If anyone will not work, neither let him eat." He went on to say that any who are "leading an undisciplined life doing no work at all," should "work in quiet fashion and eat their own bread" (2 Thes. 3:10-12). If you're physically able only to care for yourself, you can take pride in that simple fact.

There's such a thing as making life too easy for ourselves— or our parents. It's a great disservice to say to a healthy 60-year-old, "You take it easy now, Mother, we'll do all the work." She may have 20 or 30 years of living yet to do. Far too long to sit and watch.

The idea of age as a time to rest may be self-fulfilling. The more you rest, the more you may have to rest. You need to forget about age. When someone steps forward to do a job, don't ask how old he is. Let him do it. At any age we all need to be needed, to be active, to be involved. By work we pay our admission to get into the pool, to be in the delightful swim of life.

I visited an old lady in her home not long before she died. It was a simple little house but fresh and well-kept. "I am busy just taking care of myself. I like to keep my house and myself clean." That's work. If she did it, someone else didn't have to. She was no burden to her children, her neighbors, or her church deacon board.

I heard of another older woman recently, once a gracious lady, who was knocked to pieces by losses. She first gave up going to church, or going anywhere. Then she gave up taking care of her home. Relatives came in to do it. Then she gave up taking care of herself. Now she's in a mental hospital, refusing to keep herself clean. A pitiful object.

Angelo Patri said, "Education consists in being afraid at the right time." All the studies of gerontologists point to the fact that we need to keep struggling to do whatever work we can. We need to keep contributing all the effort we can to help carry the world's burden of work. We need to be afraid that if we don't use our abilities, we'll lose them.

A vigorous 65-year-old may feel stunned by the gap between his abilities and what the world expects of him. He dare not let that expectation shape him. The idea of retirement as a time of rest gives a false and misleading picture.

Continuing to Work

Dorothy Morrison at 78 works full-time as a legal secretary. Small and wiry, she hasn't changed much in looks in the 27 years I've known her. "I enjoy working," she says. "I have no retirement goals. I feel working has kept me young. I'm the oldest in the office, but I'm in contact with the young and middle-aged. Through the years I've acquired enormous knowledge. I began as law secretary with the senior partner of the firm and then quit when Kenny was born. When Kenny went away to college, I got a job. One day I happened to meet my first boss on the street and he asked if I'd be willing to come back. So he fired two girls and I took over both their jobs, managing the office and being a legal secretary. Now I'm working for his son. They keep giving me raises and bonuses. Recently they told me, 'You can work till you're 90 if you want to.' I've missed only four days for illness in the past 22 years. My husband says he won't retire till I do—he still has his own law office. So we just keep on working."

Lowell Stellberger, a lawyer, says, "At age 65 I retired from the insurance company where I was doing legal work, because I wanted to reduce my load. But I wanted to keep practicing law. Now my private practice has grown so much that I'm doing essentially just what I've been doing for the past 25 years. I do take four or five weeks off a year. I make every business trip a vacation, take Helen along, relax, see the sights. I'd like to have more time for myself. But working helps me to stay in a good mental state. The young people working for me keep my mind active. In the final analysis, I have to take responsibility for all the cases that come to us, so I have to keep ahead of them."

Retirement

People who are self-employed, or who work for small companies, can go on working. But about half of American workers are employed by companies with compulsory retirement policies. For those whose jobs bring self-realization, retirement can feel like a body blow. For others doing backbreaking labor or tedious assembly-line jobs, retirement can't come too soon.

Some people exult in retirement as a time to play, to rest, or to embark on new ventures. For others, again in both categories, retirement can be a disaster.

Why do some people want to play and others want to work in their later years? One minister's wife, mother of eight children, worked far beyond her strength through the Depression and World War II. Always pinched for money, she experienced no letup, no time to play. Once the children were raised, she played. She couldn't face cooking, so she and her husband had a hot meal brought in each day. After a few years he took over the cooking.

A minister, apparently a frustrated scholar, spent his retirement years working on a Ph.D. degree.

Retirement may be a time to make up for losses of the past. Bart and I think the ideal arrangement is a lifelong program of learning, working, playing. Learning shouldn't stop with school. Play shouldn't stop with childhood. Work shouldn't stop with adulthood. In the middle years when we're loaded with work we should still keep learning. We should also get the relaxation and recreation we need to keep emotionally in balance. Then we'll want to keep on working till the end of life—up to the limit of our ability and strength. I don't notice anything in the Bible about quitting work at a set age. We need to prepare ourselves psychologically to keep on picking up our share of the tab.

More than half of all people over 65 are physically able to work, and many more could work if jobs were modified to fit their physical conditions, says Dr. Robert Butler, authority on aging. Some firms have the idea that older people present problems as workers. But this belief is one of those myths. The fact is, they often show better work records than the young. Studies show that older people have less absenteeism, lower accident rates, greater stability, steadier rate of production, higher accuracy rates, higher quality of work, plus lower turnover. Only in laboring occupations requiring much physical strength have they shown lower performance.

Yet all too often people begin to face age discrimination at age 45. Dr. Robert Butler puts "ageism" alongside racism and sexism as a prejudice to be fought. He says retirement itself is a form of age bias, that there is no scientific data to support arbitrary retirement on the basis of age.

In our culture, social esteem depends to a great extent on productivity. The one who does not produce may feel useless. If he's viewed as a weight to be borne, he can't help knowing it. People still in good health react badly to feeling useless. Some do what they can to find new work.

Mel Butler, a man in our church, was retired as an engineer from one of the car companies at age 62. Dignified of manner, tall and distinguished looking, he got a part-time job with a funeral director. He worked several days a week, whenever needed, until he died. He loved people and was a gracious presence in the funeral home, kindly, helpful, comforting.

Former President Herbert Hoover served on his last presidential commission in 1953-55, until he was 81. He said,

There is no joy to be had from retirement except by some kind of productive work. Otherwise, you degenerate into talking to everybody about your pains and pills and income tax. Any oldster who keeps at even part-time work has something worthwhile talking about. He has zest for the morning paper and his three meals a day. The point of all this is not to retire from work or you will shrivel up into a nuisance to all mankind.

When people had their own shops, worked their own land, they worked until they were disabled or died. Today, 80 percent of all those who work are in the employ of others. The idea of retirement began in Germany in the 1880s as a humanitarian move. It became established in the U.S. after passage of the Social Security Act in 1935. The age for beginning to draw Social Security payments was arbitrarily set at 65 for men, and 62 for women. Companies came to adopt 65 as the cutoff point for their older workers. Many people had been so overworked that they were happy enough to retire. The problems of having nothing to do hit them afterward.

Some who retire at the height of success suffer what psychologists call "success depression." Poets call it "the melancholy of all things completed." After these people have arrived, they discover that the fun was in the struggle. We discovered this after a 13-year pastorate, when we suddenly saw that all our dreams for that church had been realized. Then there was nothing to do but move on to another hard job. Now we don't plan on ever being through. We keep some dreams always ahead.

Blue-collar workers who don't find satisfaction in their jobs transfer their dreams to something outside the job. They dream of owning a home or a small business or a boat, of attaining security, or of educating their children or themselves. After retirement they may pursue dreams of a garden, building or remodeling a home. We all need work. It's a terrible thing for an old person to feel that all his plans have been either carried out or abandoned, that nothing requires his presence any longer.

New Forms of Work

It has been said that the average life expectancy of a commercial pilot who is forced to retire is 32 months. If he sits on a bench, feels like a nobody, has no friends, no goals, no work, he's finished. Retirement calls for new forms of work. We all need structure to our lives, something that requires us to get out of bed in the morning.

When Margaret Parsons reached retirement years, she found she needed to supplement her income. She didn't feel she could handle a nine-to-five job. A couple asked her to stay in their home and supervise two teenage children while they vacationed. She found she liked being a live-in grandma for a short time, and applied for more work of the same kind through a specialized employment agency. The work took her into very wealthy homes, where she acted as a kind of governess to schoolage children. She also supervised workers who came in and out of the home to do routine jobs.

Her qualifications and availability have spread by word of mouth, and she no longer needs the agency. She has been an adoptive grandmother to a number of young people. Often she has bound up the bleeding hearts of youngsters suffering various traumas, including divorce of their parents.

We all need our hill country to conquer. It was on his 85th birthday that Caleb put in his bid to Joshua for a harder job:

> And now behold, the Lord has let me live, just as He spoke, these 45 years, from the time that the Lord spoke this word to Moses, when Israel walked in the wilderness; and now behold, I am 85 years old today. I am still as strong today as I was in the day Moses sent me; as my strength was then, so my strength is now, for war and for going out and coming in. Now then,

give me this hill country about which the Lord spoke on that day . . ." (Josh. 14:10-12).

All those years in the wilderness Caleb had carried his dream. He wanted to conquer a most difficult portion of the country. The spies 40 years before had turned away in fear of giants and walled towns. Caleb said, "Perhaps the Lord will be with me, and I shall drive them out" (v. 12). He succeeded.

Any number of people past 65 feel like Caleb, "I am still as strong today as I was," and they want work to do. About 40 percent of those over 65 who are working are self-employed. Some are in agriculture, others work as real-estate agents, income-tax preparers, answering-service operators, seamstresses, typists, gardeners, caterers, craftsmen, carpenters, repairmen, baby-sitters, small shop and restaurant owners. One retired man joined his wife's catering business.

Older people are thought to have lost a bit in creativity. But look around you, read the magazines and papers. Any number of people have done their best work in later years. Look at politicians and government leaders. Look at entertainers, musicians, actors and actresses. Many of them embark on new projects after age 65.

Creative work may be raising beautiful vegetables in a garden. Bill Logie often comes to our door with gorgeous offerings of strawberries, sweet corn, tomatoes, squash. One time he furnished strawberries for shortcake for a church dinner of 250 people. Don't tell him that didn't involve work. He beams with pride at the beauty of his produce. He's 79. I don't think he ever gets up in the morning and thinks, "I'm too old to be of any use." From early spring to late fall he works from two to six hours a day in his garden.

Lincoln wrote of himself as "old and withered" at age 48, two years before he was elected president. After that he didn't speak of his age—apparently, he was too busy.

The later years can be a glorious time of having come to terms with what we have accomplished, what we will never accomplish. Of accepting and making the most of ourselves—through work.

Against almost overwhelming odds, almost one-third of the income of older people comes from current earnings. If not self-employed, they may work part-time in unskilled service occupations. But they work. There's always need for custodians, watchmen, waitresses, practical nurses.

To work, we can't be afraid of new things. We can't use old age as an excuse for nonperformance. We have to be willing sometimes, as a young athlete describes it, to "play over pain." Sometimes we have to figure we won't feel any worse working than not working, so we might as well work.

Getting Today's Work Done

How do you get your work done, either on the job or if self-employed? Francis Bacon said:

> *Men of age object too much, consult too long, adventure too little, repent too soon, and seldom drive business home to the full period, but content themselves with a mediocrity of success.*

Certainly we need to learn the disciplines necessary to accomplish the projects we have in mind. It's difficult to learn new things. I had said I didn't want a microwave oven, because friends told me it involved learning a whole new method of cooking. I thought, "I'll finish out my days cooking the way I'm used to. I don't want to learn a different way." Then some people gave me one and I had to learn to use it. It took two weeks to get up my nerve to touch it. I read the book, went to a few classes, and now I use it all the time. I feel so up-to-date!

Now Bart says I'm to get a minicomputer word processor and learn to use it. I will, I promise—but not right now—not till I get this book written. The typewriter is so comfortable, so familiar . . . I'd have to go to classes, I'd have to learn a new way of doing. But I will, I promise.

My teenage grandsons work out problems and play games on computers. It would be good for me to learn. As the preacher says in Ecclesiastes, "The race is not to the swift, or the battle to the strong" (9:11, NIV). We don't need to let the world move past us.

Years ago, one of our children asked, "Mom, which do you think is harder—yours and Daddy's jobs, or my job of going to school?" Then he answered his own question, "I think my job is harder, because you know how to do what you're doing, and I have to learn new things all the time."

If you want to keep the spirit of youth, you have to keep learning new things—all your life. Changing, adjusting, moving forward. Scripture exhorts us to work, make an effort, struggle, plan ahead (Prov. 10:4-5; 14:23; 19:15; 20:4; 21:5, 25-26; 22:13).

> Is your place a small place?
> Tend it with care;
> He set you there.
>
> Is your place a large place?
> Guard it with care!
> He set you there.
>
> Whate'er your place, it is
> Not yours alone, but his
> Who set you there.
> ("Work," John Oxenham)

*F*IVE *❧*:
SERVICE—
Are You Exercising
Your Gift?

Service is the rent you pay for the space you occupy.

As recently as 1900, only 4 percent of the population of the U.S. was over 65, as compared to almost 12 percent in 1983. In 1900, an older person stood out for his sheer survival. Contagious disease carried away many at every stage of life. Today there are over 32,000 people 100 years of age or older in the U.S. A 70-year-old is still in the youth of old age.

Since 1950, the 65-and-over age group has grown more than twice as fast as the population under 65. We don't want those under 65 to feel inundated by oldsters. Prejudice increases with the numbers in any given group. The sheer number of us could increase age prejudice. We don't dare go around talking about how old we are, claiming privileges and exemptions.

The best idea is to forget about age and try to pass as a member of the community. Bart's mother, teaching Bible classes around New York City till age 87, refused to let anyone know her age. "If they knew how old I was, they wouldn't make any plans. They'd think I was going to die tomorrow." You'll be treasured, as she was, if you make a business of meeting people's needs.

Jesus stated an age-old principle of human relations—"Give, and it will be given to you; good measure, pressed down, shaken together, running over, they will pour into your lap. For whatever measure you deal out to others, it will be dealt to you in return" (Luke 6:38). If you want a lot back, just start giving. Give money, give time, give effort, give yourself. It will all come back—like seed planted—a hundredfold. Service in the family, in the church, in the community is the most self-serving thing in the world. It's a privilege you don't dare miss—for your own good.

It's one of those myths of old age that senior citizens prefer to disengage from life and withdraw into themselves. You and the rest of the population of older people can easily explode that myth. Withdrawal is only one of many patterns of reaction to advancing years. Today, some of the busiest people in church and community are past age 65. You don't think about their age because they're as eager to be involved as people of any other age group. When she was 92, Gertrude Rutgers had a serious operation on her leg. We feared she was finished, that we'd have to get someone else to handle the sale of over 500 study books for one of my classes but she's back—insisting she can do it.

Studies show that active interest in anything will improve your health and prolong your life. But it is better to get involved in things that need doing long before you reach retirement age. Said Seneca, "Nothing is more disgraceful than that an old man should have nothing to show to prove that he has lived long, except his years."

Fruit in Old Age
The Bible promises that if we plant our lives in the right

places we'll produce fruit in old age.

> The righteous man will flourish like the palm tree,
> He will grow like a cedar in Lebanon.
> Planted in the house of the Lord,
> They will flourish in the courts of our God.
> They will still yield fruit in old age;
> They shall be full of sap and very green,
> To declare that the Lord is upright (Ps. 92:12-15).

When God promised through the Prophet Joel to pour out His Spirit upon all mankind, He specifically included the elderly. He said old men were to "dream dreams." We need to keep our vision fresh and never give up our dreams for carrying out some new aspect of God's work.

When Gene Jordan retired from business, he had a dream of devoting more time to the Lord's work. He attends church or Bible classes four times a week, "serving the body of Christ by my presence." He makes himself available for any need. "Only this morning I was called from the worship service to teach a third-grade class whose teacher was absent. One of my gifts is to serve the Lord on very short notice. I find myself Spirit-filled for the occasion." He tries to be sensitive to people's needs, and finds it rewarding to drive people to the hospital or doctor's office, to take them shopping and out to eat. He changes windows and screens, washes windows—wherever there is need. "I thank God for the strength to do these things in Christian love," he says.

Many seize upon retirement as a time to be like Anna, the prophetess. At 84, "she never left the temple, serving night and day with fastings and prayers" (Luke 2:37).

George Mielke shows up at the church every weekday at about 9 A.M. He brings a lunch and works for four or five hours in the Media Center, running off copies of sermons on tape, and helping with records. Sometimes he does big jobs in the office, like labeling boxes of church envelopes. He may run errands, replace broken asphalt tile, or glue chairs back together. Sometimes he goes to widows' homes to take care of heating problems. A young housewife asked if she could pay him to do some handyman jobs for her. "If you pay, I won't do it," he said.

On Sundays George gets to church at 7:45 A.M. to make coffee for nearly three hours before he attends the third service. He says this started with his own adult class, gradually expanded to include the other adult classes, the Christian education people—anyone who wants a cup of coffee, tea, or hot chocolate. Lots of people, he says, stay the whole morning—teaching, attending a class, going to a service—and they need refreshment. It all adds up to around 1,000 cups a Sunday. To pay for all this, he sets out a little basket for anyone who wants to make a contribution. The expense is more than covered.

A Cause that Will Outlast Us

"The great use of life is to spend it for something that will outlast it," said William James, the psychologist. We all carry a huge debt through life for all we've been given in childhood, youth, and adulthood. Paul wrote to the Romans, "Let no debt remain outstanding, except the continuing debt to love one another" (Rom. 13:8, NIV). We'll never get that debt of love paid off, nor would we want to. The joy is in the giving. With the giving comes receiving, and so we are in relationship with a wealth of people.

As the years go on, we become aware that a deadline looms ahead. Time is too short for all we want to do. Jesus said, "As long as it is day, we must do the work of Him who sent Me. Night is coming, when no one can work" (John 9:4, NIV).

Hayward and "Mother" Crawford are a couple who feel

that sense of urgency. Hayward at 86 serves as full-time pastor of a black church in downtown Detroit. He came to Detroit as a boy of 17 before World War I. He worked in factories, went into business for himself as a cement contractor until that ended in the Depression. He then realized his "true calling," attended Bible college, and has now been in the ministry for 50 years.

"There's no retiring in this work," he says. He preaches almost every Sunday, studies people to know their problems, temperaments, and needs. Most problems in the church, he thinks, come from misunderstanding the basic purpose of the church—to bring people to Jesus Christ. "I'm the oldest thing around—our people range from teenagers to 50 years of age. Every Wednesday night 35 to 50 people come to study the Bible. These people love each other in spite of poverty and unemployment."

Hayward's wife says the people support them as they can. "They give us a gift whether we need it or not. Last week I was given a bushel of string beans—one whole bushel. Sunday a woman brought me some frozen stuff—and I have no freezer. Members on food stamps say they have no money, but give a few food stamps. Several months ago someone gave me 35 pounds of cheese—and I'm on a salt-free diet. But I feel the love that comes with the gifts and I appreciate them.

"I'm called 'Mother Crawford'—have been for the past 35 years. I do all the little things that nobody else wants to do. I can understand the problems of being poor because I've never been anything else. I do a lot of speaking—last week I spoke at a Bible conference in Chicago.

"I came from Alabama, and used to do housework for people when the church didn't pay. I learned to talk like the people in those houses talked. You just pick it up, you know.

"Now I do my own housework, weed my yard, even

though I have high blood pressure. It has to be done, so I do it.

"My husband and I read the Bible every day, we've read it through 36 times. In my classes I read five chapters a week, explain sometimes, tie up with other verses, apply to their lives. I get a lot of unwed mothers, mothers on ADC. They memorize verses every week, letter perfect, and receive a little award at the end of the year for doing so. Each week they teach the verses to their children. I give the Word, the Lord waters it.

"I have 4 children, 14 grandchildren, and 5 great-grandchildren. Cooking is what I do best—everyone eats at this table. Growing up, there were 14 of us. 'Just put another cup of water in the gravy and another plate on the table,' my mother used to say when we had a guest. That's the way I entertain. I never apologize, I just share what I have.

"I'm surprised that someone told you I was old. I never think about being old. I'm too busy."

We all need a cause that will outlast us. Then all our little efforts count, up to the very end.

Living Epistles
God says we're to be living letters of Christ, written for all men to read (2 Cor. 3:2-3).

It's easy to depend upon a position—what you do—for your sense of identity. In retirement, what you *are* is more important than what you *do*. You can serve other people simply as an example. Walt Whitman wrote:

> Youth, large, lusty, loving—
> youth full of grace, force, fascination,
> Do you know that Old Age may come after you
> with equal grace, force, fascination?

Growing older with style means selecting what is consistent with you as an individual. You have a lot inside, and you'll express that depth in ways that are peculiarly your own. You'll be different, distinct, of your own special flavor. You can minister—serve—by demonstrating how Christ meets your needs, how He makes life rich and beautiful.

> As a white candle
> In a holy place,
> So is the beauty
> Of an aged face.
> (Joseph Campbell, "The Old Woman")

The Bible gives a clear picture of what older people are to be. "Older men are to be temperate, dignified, sensible, sound in faith, in love, in perseverance. Older women likewise are to be reverent in their behavior, not malicious gossips, nor enslaved to much wine" (Titus 2:2-5).

The sight of older people in the streets is to be one of the blessings of the kingdom age (Zech. 8:4). Only under good conditions can people survive to old age.

When Bart and I were quite young we served a newly forming church. With no one over 40 in that church, we felt a distinct lack. No one served as an example of what long years of walking and talking with God can produce.

Declaring God's Power
People who have walked with God for a lifetime can declare God's power with particular effectiveness. Wally Hostetter, one of our associate pastors, did a lot of work with patients in a nursing home when he was in seminary. These people suffer multiple physical problems. Yet he found they could be encouraged to serve God by ministering to each other. Doing so carries them beyond their own problems.

One person he met inspired him greatly. "Finding one

saint like Ella Jordan helped me through some depressing times when I felt there would be little or no results to my ministry in the nursing home. I was walking past her room when I heard some Gospel preaching coming from the radio. I looked in and saw a woman leaning over with her head almost in her lap, next to the radio. As she raised her head, I saw that she was blind. I sat down and told her I was studying to be a preacher. Her face lit up and she asked if I had a Bible. She put her hands on the Bible and asked me to pray for her. She joined in excitedly. At that time, and afterward when I visited her, when I'd start to read Scripture, she'd almost always recite the passage from memory. Visiting her was a great pickup for me."

The greater the handicaps and suffering, the more powerful can be the witness for Christ. We are to be Christ's ambassadors (2 Cor. 5:20). We're not exempted because of age (Ps. 148:12-13). We can ask God to keep us in old age, to enable us to declare His strength to our generation, His power to those yet to come (Ps. 71:9, 18).

We can ask the Lord to postpone weakness until we have accomplished what He wants us to do for Him. I've looked at people who spare themselves, and others who keep struggling against all odds. The strugglers seem to do better. Sometimes I'm not bursting with energy to get out and teach my weekly Bible classes. But I remind myself that 30 years ago I wasn't always bursting with energy to do what I really wanted to do. And at present I'm going along better than I was then. "My power is made perfect in weakness" (2 Cor. 12:9, NIV). We don't need to make an excuse of age. God will give us the energy when we need it to get through what we want to do for Him.

What Can You Do?
All of us need to be needed, and many need what we can give. "We who are strong ought to bear with the failings of

the weak and not to please ourselves" (Rom. 15:1, NIV).

■ Listening. Strength comes in various capacities. You may be strong emotionally, and weak physically. You may be able to offer a tremendous ministry of listening. You don't need a degree in psychotherapy to make your efforts count. Psychologist Bernie Zilbergeld has written a book, *The Shrinking of America.* In this book he surveys the vast number of studies on the effects of psychotherapy. His conclusion: the chief benefit of therapy seems to come from talking to a sympathetic listener. Do professionals generally get better results than amateur advisors? Says Zilbergeld, "The answer, hard as it may be to accept, is that they don't." He goes on to say, "The most common products of most therapies are not behavior changes, but caring, comforting, and structuring."

Common sense, sensitivity, the wisdom of age, and a knowledge of the Bible can make you the minister of healing when someone on your block, someone in your family, someone in your church, needs help.

■ Teaching. Older people can teach—not only people their own age but all ages (1 Cor. 12:28—"teachers"; Rom. 12:7—"teaching"). Remember, nobody wants to listen to what you learned years ago. You can build on past knowledge and experience, but people want to hear about what you've learned this week.

Older women are to teach what is good, encourage young women to love their husbands and children, be sensible, pure, workers at home, kind, subject to their own husbands—"that the Word of God may not be dishonored" (Titus 2:3-5). A young woman in a small Bible study said, "I don't want to be in a group with others only of my own age. Older women help us so much to see our problems in perspective."

Older men as well as women in our church help in the nurseries, teach and help in Vacation Bible School. Little

folks love a grandfather image and some don't have grand-
fathers of their own (see 1 Cor. 12:28—"helps"; Rom.
12:7— "service").

■ Administration. Some older people have tremendous
skills in administration. Those with this gift can serve in
many capacities, both active and consultative. I think of a
few aged saints throughout Bart's ministry whom he turned
to often as consultants. If we restrain ourselves from drown-
ing people with advice, and let them know they don't have
to follow our recommendations, they will ask. It's delightful
to be asked. We will be, if we resist the impulse to control
(see 1 Cor. 12:8—"wisdom"; 12:28—"administrations").

No one is better equipped to set up and carry on a church
ministry to older people than a strong older person. He can
be a living example and inspiration, a testimonial of what
God can do. He can put his developed skills to use. He can
also discover and bring out hitherto unrealized strengths in
other older people. The important thing is to provide real
challenge—not busywork. The world needs the efforts of
these people. Activities should be planned to glorify God
and build up individuals. Fellowship can be based on Bible
study, with other supporting activities.

Possibilities for activities include monthly fellowship
dinners, weekly shopping trips to certain stores, weekly
home delivery of groceries, a co-op run by the elderly to
keep down the cost of food, a barter exchange of talents
and services, tours and outings, a cooperative garage sale to
reduce home inventory.

Retirees can help others weather the adjustments of retirement. No one is better able to give help than those who
have successfully maneuvered the passage.

■ Hospitality. Many older people have themselves been
enriched through a ministry of hospitality. Think, for example, of the many foreign students who come to this
country for an education. Every one of them goes back to

his country as a leader. Most feel very lonely here. By mothering, or fathering, by offering a home away from home, you might strengthen one such student in his Christian faith, or lead him to Christ. If so, you'd be doing more than going abroad as a missionary yourself. He has the foreign culture down pat. And that's the hardest thing of all for a missionary to take on. "Do not neglect to show hospitality to strangers, for by this some have entertained angels without knowing it" (Heb. 13:2).

We can show hospitality even with limited space and means if we learn the difference between biblical hospitality and secular entertaining. It's the difference between simply sharing what we have and are, and desiring to impress. When we give up our selfish pride, everything becomes easy. "Be hospitable to one another without complaint" (1 Peter 4:9).

■ Artistry. One who loves beauty can exercise his special gift through planting flowers, setting up displays, making table decorations (see Ex. 35:25-26, 30-35; Rom. 12:7— "service"; 1 Cor. 12:28—"helps"). We can witness to the world through expressing God's love of beauty.

■ Phone checks. Even the weakest and most limited person can do something. Someone at home could help in a checkup telephone service—to call people who live alone to check on their well-being, summon help if needed, or simply call people more lonely than themselves. A single phone call or card or note can reverberate through one's whole day and beyond.

■ Home nursing. Some with gifts of healing could help in home nursing, paid for out of the deacon's fund, if necessary.

■ Prayer. An invalid can carry on a ministry of prayer for others, keeping track of God's answers to prayer, whether "Yes," "No", or "Wait."

■ Outreach. Activities for seniors should have the same

thrust as the program for any other age group. Not only what can I do to grow, but what can I do to contribute? We grow not only through learning but through doing. The urgency of something that needs to be done for someone else can propel us into action. It can keep us learning and growing.

Giving can move outside the church too. Enormous community needs face us—teaching disadvantaged children to read, working for political candidates whose principles we support, or helping in hospitals or schools or universities. Jesus said, "It's more blessed to give than to receive" (Acts 20:35). We haven't really matured until we've discovered that for ourselves. When we give something, anything, we feel strengthened, enlarged, more than repaid. We get more than we give.

> *If I can stop one heart from breaking,*
> *I shall not live in vain;*
> *If I can ease one life the aching,*
> *Or cool one pain,*
> *Or help one fainting robin*
> *Into his nest again,*
> *I shall not live in vain.*
>
> (Emily Dickinson)

Giving Your Gifts
The whole business of doing, doing, doing is a drag unless you've figured out what's right for you to do. Don't let people talk you into doing jobs just to get them done. If necessary, help find the right person. But don't load yourself up with things you don't want to do. Ask the Holy Spirit to help you find your gift. You won't get anything worthwhile done if you don't learn to say no to things that aren't for you. Eliminate, eliminate, eliminate. Relegate the machinery of life to the realm of habit as much as possible.

On the other hand, try everything once. Don't narrow your interests until you've shut yourself out of life. Bart and I had agreed that those river float trips through rough water weren't for us. Then last summer in Alaska he came back to our hotel room in Juneau saying he had bought two tickets for a float trip down the river of the Mendenhall Glacier. I knew it would be cold, I didn't have waterproof clothing, I felt worried at the prospect. But we're both committed to trying new things. I didn't offer a word of objection, just went along. And sure enough when we got to the spot on the riverbank to get into the little dinghy, we were equipped with rubber boots and ponchos. We bounced around through the rapids, saw some beautiful scenery for several hours, got wet—and survived! No colds or sore throats. We don't plan on any more float trips, but we feel really good that we managed that one. Trying new experiences keeps alive the spirit of adventure.

On a more serious level, you'll only discover your true gifts by trying many things. It's a new experience for a retired executive to help in the church nursery. Some love it. "As each one has received a special gift, employ it in serving one another, as good stewards of the manifold grace of God" (1 Peter 4:10).

The Bible makes clear that no one gift is more important than another. "The members of the body which seem to be weaker are necessary" (1 Cor. 12:22). You need a liver even more than you need eyes. The person who repairs the broken chairs is part of the church body. He has a ministry just as important in the sight of God as the one who stands in the pulpit.

Keep trying different kinds of ministry until you find the thing that is fun for you to do. When you make that discovery, the sense of sacrificing your time and your energy will evaporate. You'll find it all joy. You'll find yourself through service.

SIX ✿ FRIENDS— What to Do About Them

There are wonders in true affection . . . wherein two so become one, as they both become two.

Sir Thomas Browne,
Religio Medici, part II, sec. 6

Friends cost you money and take your time. They may move away or die. And sometimes they just plain disappoint you. So why bother?

The Bible gives a lot of reasons why we need friends. "Two are better than one because they have a good return for their labor" (Ecc. 4:9). Work becomes fun when someone comes over to help. Two men can have a good time finishing a basement, or building on an extra room together. Two women have a great time canning applesauce or hanging wallpaper together.

We need friends in times of trouble or illness. "For if either of them falls, the one will lift up his companion. But woe to the one who falls when there is not another to lift him up" (Ecc. 4:10).

We need friends to strengthen us against common adversaries. "And if one can overpower him who is alone, two can resist him. A cord of three strands is not quickly torn apart" (Ecc. 4:12). We clump together in churches and other organizations to find strength for ourselves.

We need friends to see ourselves more clearly. A friend helps us find our own identity. "As in water face reflects face, so the heart of man reflects man" (Prov. 27:19). A friend helps us appreciate half-hidden aptitudes in ourselves. A friend defines us by relating to or echoing certain qualities we scarcely see or appreciate in ourselves. A friend can help us set realistic goals.

We need friends to guard us from error. A friend tells us when we're wrong, or when we need to change course. One time a friend told me why my Bible classes were going down. I was suffering through an illness in the family that was too devastating to talk about in public. She told me I wasn't using enough personal illustrations. My teaching was becoming too detached, too academic. She took the trouble to tell me what was wrong, rather than let me be further devastated by seeing my classes slip away. "Faithful are the wounds of a friend, but deceitful are the kisses of an enemy" (Prov. 27:6).

We need friends for talking over plans and problems. "Oil and perfume make the heart glad, so a man's counsel is sweet to his friend" (Prov. 27:9). We need a sounding board, someone to come up with another point of view, someone to help us think through a situation.

We need friends to stimulate us, to challenge us to grow. "Iron sharpens iron, so one man sharpens another" (Prov. 27:17).

A college friend of mine wrote in a letter, "I hang onto friends as a squirrel hides nuts." I appreciate the way she's hung onto me, through all the busy years. Emerson said,

> We take care of our health; we lay up money; we make
> our roof tight, and our clothing sufficient; but who
> provides wisely that he shall not be wanting in the best
> property of all—friends? ("Conduct of Life: Consider-
> ations by the Way").

Shylock, in Shakespeare's *Merchant of Venice,* said plain-
tively, "I would be friends with you and have your love"
(Act I, Sc. 3, 1.139). We all want and need friends—
whatever the risks in friendship.

The Risk of Friendship

It's not smart to carry all your eggs in one basket. When the
Washington Public Power Supply System defaulted on its
bonds, a woman was shown on television saying, "We lost
our entire retirement income—$135,000. We had invested
all of it in WPPSS." Didn't anyone ever tell her to spread
the risk?

In friendships, you don't dare invest everything even in a
husband or wife. Death or illness can knock down that
all-important person. You need to spread the risk not only
over various individuals, but over various age groups.

Younger friends who treat you like a peer are delightful—
they make you feel young. It's fun sharing confidences,
dreaming dreams, sharing goals together. They help you to
look ahead. You're less likely to lose young friends through
death.

Vernon and Vidie Patterson of Charlotte, North Caro-
lina are rich in young friends. When you see them, it's hard
to believe they're in their 90s. "We've been married 62
years. The other evening an engaged couple came over to
talk to us about our married life. They stayed from 6 to 10
o'clock.

"Another evening this week a bride and bridegroom and three engaged couples came. We told them funny things and serious things. They all stayed till 10 o'clock."

Vidie spoke of the daughter of her one-time best friend. "Martha called up and said she wanted to stay overnight with us. I said there wasn't room, the guest room was occupied. She said, 'Oh, you have room. I'll just sleep on the couch in that little back room.' And she did."

Vidie mentioned such a great number of young friends that I asked, "Do you have any few specially close friends?"

She said quickly, "My close friends, the ones who were like sisters, have all gone to be with the Lord. Pat has one close friend left." She hurried on to say, "But their daughters now come to see us. It's not hard to have friends."

Vidie Patterson says she bakes cookies for the neighborhood children, and has many little friends who come to call.

We don't dare invest all of our capacity for friendship in our contemporaries. "After a certain distance, every step we take in life we find the ice growing thinner below our feet, and all around us and behind us we see our contemporaries going through" (Stevenson, *Virginibus Puerisque: Aes Triplex*).

We need friends among children for many reasons. Jesus insisted that His disciples let the little children come close to Him. Another time He called a child, stood him in their midst and said,

Unless you are converted and become like children, you shall not enter the kingdom of heaven. Whoever then humbles himself as this child, he is the greatest in the kingdom of heaven. And whoever receives one such child in My name receives Me (Matt. 18:2-5).

We can learn so much from children. We see the world

afresh through their eyes—the beauty of a pansy, the wonder of the Big Dipper. We can experience with them the joy of learning and discovering at museums, in the woods, at the seashore. It's easy to make contacts with children, whether you have grandchildren or not. In an apartment building where we started our married life, two maiden ladies "adopted" our two-year-old. Any parent is delighted with an offer of baby-sitting.

One Sunday Bart and I agreed to baby-sit two grandsons who were three and five. We had planned on a two-and-one-half-mile nature walk in the woods that day, to enjoy the fall colors. We feared we'd have to give that up, but decided to go anyway and see how far we'd get. The two boys, excited by the adventure, ran the entire course! We had to hurry to keep up. It was fun sharing the experience with them.

Along with new friends and young friends, of course we need old friends. None of us want to give up old friends till we have to. We like to be with those to whom we're forever young, because they knew us when.

> To me, fair friend, you never can be old,
>   For as you were when first your eye I eyed,
> Such seems your beauty still.
>   Shakespeare (Sonnet civ)

Finding Friends

Should you exercise discernment in friends or be a friend to anyone who comes along? Both. We grow with friends to whom we have to stretch to relate—friends entirely different from ourselves, different backgrounds, different interests, as well as different ages. Sometimes true friends are complementary. We enjoy something in the other which is lacking in ourselves.

We can admit anybody to whatever degree of friendship

we have time and energy for. We can grow through helping someone who needs our help. But we do need discernment. As parents we watch our children carefully to see how various friendships affect them. Some youngsters pull them up, others pull them down.

Likewise, we need to keep an eye on what any particular relationship is doing to us. "Do not associate with a man given to anger; or go with a hot-tempered man, lest you learn his ways, and find a snare for yourself" (Prov. 22:24-25). Sometimes fat people want to associate only with fat people, angry people with angry people, rebels with rebels, lazy people with lazy. Watch it! Be discerning. We need people different from ourselves, as well as those who are like us.

Look at Jesus and His friendships. The Pharisees accused Him of keeping company with publicans and sinners. It's all a question of who influences whom. Jesus could go anywhere and change the whole atmosphere. We may not be so strong. But the ideal is to grow strong enough—spiritually, emotionally—to be a friend to anyone who needs us. We should discourage attitudes of fussiness or exclusiveness in ourselves or our children.

Cicero, the Roman statesman and philosopher, stated that complete unity of aim is the traditional condition of genuine and sincere friendship. Some of the most wonderful friendships of all develop where God uses us to bring one another into complete unity of aim in Christ.

Karen Jackson, assistant in our singles ministry, defines friendship well. "If you seek only the comfort zone in friendships, from babyhood on, your life will narrow more and more. If you go for surmounting the comfort zone, for facing hard things, you'll build character. Going for character development will draw you into relationships that won't be easy. But they'll help you to grow. Challenging relationships will become more and more comfortable. You expand your comfort zone in the process of relating to people different from yourself. If you insist on friendship only with those exactly like yourself in age and background, you shrink your comfort zone. You'll find yourself comfortable with fewer and fewer people."

Being a Friend

"The greatest myth about friendship is that it will come to people without their doing something in exchange for it," says Eugene Kennedy, professor of psychology at Loyola University, Chicago. "People believe that others will respond to them automatically. They feel entitled to affection and friendship. They seem to say, 'Payment is due me.'"

If you want friends, you have to be a friend. You won't have friends unless you offer something for exchange in the marketplace of life. That may sound crass to you, but it's a fact. Friendship implies a two-way transaction. Jesus, the greatest Friend of all, laid down His life for us. "Greater love has no one than this, that one lay down his life for his friends" (John 15:13). To be His friend, we have to give something—ourselves.

Says Karen Jackson, "Being a friend means being for the other person what you long for for yourself."

Having something to exchange doesn't mean only looks or wealth. Some say that making friends becomes harder as our looks fade. But we've all seen another kind of beauty emerge in some persons. Said a young man to a woman nearing 70, "You are aging so beautifully. You get better looking all the time. It's really neat."

For the sake of our friends and family, I think we should make the very most of whatever looks God has given us— by diet, exercise, posture, grooming, appropriate clothes. Out of simple consideration, why not be as easy as we can on people's eyes? It's not just for yourself that you go to all that effort. It's a kindness to those you love. It's the outward evidence of a disciplined life. One older woman said to another who was wearing a suit she liked, "It's positively a public service to wear such a good-looking suit." Keeping up your appearance makes it easier for people to get to the real you. Even in illness you can be clean and neat. There's no use throwing up roadblocks to friendship.

Wealth is no necessary commodity in acquiring friends. Dr. Kennedy says that people with very great wealth or very great beauty sometimes have real trouble with friendships. They constantly suspect that others value them only for their money or their looks.

Listening

The real coin of friendship is giving of yourself. Friendship can start with listening. Friendships form when we reach down or reach up to listen. Vernon Patterson has collected innumerable friends over his lifetime. He says, "Some find it difficult to talk to people who are prominent or wealthy. Not I. I've always tried to meet people who knew more than I did—I thought some of it would rub off.

"One of my very best friends was Dr. A.T. Robertson, the great New Testament Greek scholar. These people who know so much—their great knowledge has largely separated them from other people. I approach people who are specialists in nuclear fusion, whatever, something I know absolutely nothing about. I just ask a few general questions about whatever a person is interested in. Just a general question is OK. I ask him to tell me something about it. He's learned so much, and so few people are interested in listening that he's eager to talk. That's been my practice all through life. Just show real interest. It works with very simple people too. Everyone is interested in something. Find out what it is, and then learn."

Vernon Patterson says he always turns the conversation

toward the really important things of life and eternity, and shares his faith. When his grandson went to meet him at the airport recently, he had to wait a while till Vernon finished his conversation with someone he had met on the plane. As usual, he was sharing his faith. How can he hold back from sharing the biggest thing in his life, after he's built a bridge of friendship? He doesn't find the age of 90-plus any barrier. People old and young long for someone to listen, to appreciate, to be interested in them.

Bart and I learned along the way to stop talking and to listen. Early in our ministry, I would teach a class, Bart would preach Sunday morning and evening, then we'd go out socially to someone's house and talk. Talking usually consisted of our talking, others listening. The unfairness of that hit us. These people had listened to us all day. And we weren't learning a thing by listening to ourselves. If we wanted genuine friendships, going out socially should mean listening to others, or at least an interchange.

We now have a wonderful time listening. We learn what's going on in other people's minds, and we come home feeling enriched. We've learned how to build bridges of conversation with total strangers, just by finding out what the other person does or is interested in, and then listening. Everyone knows more than we do about something.

Affirming
If you want friends, affirm. Don't judge. Be a Barnabas. Remember how Barnabas saw possibilities in Paul when no one else did? He sent for him from Antioch for that first missionary journey. Remember how Barnabas didn't give up on young Mark, even when Paul felt Mark had failed dismally? (Acts 11:19-30; 13-15)

My mother was a Barnabas. After my father died, she lived alone in her house in the town of Traer, Iowa. She said, "I'll be all right. People are always stopping in."

Why did they stop in? Because she affirmed everybody. At her funeral a friend said, "We stopped in to see your mother because she made us feel like more than we are." She could find something to appreciate in everyone. She steadfastly looked at the very best each person was capable of being. That's the way the Lord looks at us—in terms of our possibilities. That's why we should spend a lot of time with Him as a Friend.

My mother even had a friendship going with the boy next door. If she put up a red card in the window facing his house, that meant she had an errand for him to run, or something she needed him to do. He'd show up promptly. She paid him some small amount, but it was more than money that kept a busy schoolboy coming back.

Affirming people is a valuable commodity in friendship. Everyone will want to stop a minute to talk if he knows he can count on a word or an attitude of encouragement. We all need heartening.

Friendship requires that we give something. I enormously admire people who give of themselves in hospitality. I have not been able to manage such hospitality—except for my family. And sometimes I'm down in bed after one of those mighty efforts—say, entertaining 15 over Christmas.

I know that I'm the loser in the matter of hospitality. I'd like to entertain foreign students, neighbors, friends in the church—lots of people. But my energy just won't stretch that far. In the first few years of marriage I tried both hospitality and Bible teaching. But I got so much more appreciation for my teaching in relation to the energy expended, that I chose to go that direction. Ministry, I found, earns you a wealth of friends. Ministry is another word for serving and can be one end of a two-way bridge to other people. Don't forget you have to give something that other people value, if you're going to have friends.

Your life as an example can be a negotiable value in friendship. If you're a reassuring sight to younger people of what it means to grow old, they'll seek you out. Young people would rather see a sermon on how to live than hear one.

Part of my mother's charm was her attitude. When she was young, someone said to her, "Old age is pitiful." She made up her mind then to prove that old age needn't be pitiful. She cultivated the fruit of the Spirit throughout a lifetime—"love, joy, peace, patience, kindness, goodness, faithfulness, gentleness, self-control" (Gal. 5:22-23). In her autumn years she reaped the harvest in friends.

Even invalids can find this fruit of the Spirit a negotiable commodity. With it, they can still make and keep friends. People want to be in the atmosphere they create. Even ill or ailing old people can make a business of enjoying life. They can read, connect up with good programs on TV or radio, listen to people, count their blessings. They can cultivate a wide range of concerns. They can pray. A woman horribly crippled with arthritis said to me, "Life is still good." That's what people want to hear—how she manages to arrive at that conclusion despite all obstacles.

Responding to Needs

One thing friendship does require is responding promptly to needs, doing what you can. Response may mean taking someone into your home for three weeks. It may mean having lunch together, or taking in a hot meal for the family. Response sometimes means writing a note or phoning or visiting. But you must respond quickly when your friend needs you, or you won't have friends. Samuel Johnson said, "The most fatal disease of friendship is gradual decay, or dislike hourly increased by causes too slender for complaint, and too numerous for removal" (The Idler, no. 23).

On the other hand, friendship requires forgiveness. You

can't terminate a friendship every time someone fails to jump when you expect him to. Friendship requires that you not suffocate each other with demands. You need to be capable of living your own life, taking care of your own needs as much as possible, of not needing your friends too much. Friendship should allow for perfect freedom of coming or going.

Friendship requires loyalty. It requires speaking well of a friend in his absence as well as in his presence.

Taking the trouble to be interesting enhances friendship. Don't just dump a lot of mental and emotional garbage on your friend and expect him to listen because he's your friend. If you invite him for a meal, you wouldn't serve him garbage. You'd take the trouble to arrange an attractive table, and set before him good food. He deserves the same consideration in conversation. You can't serve a good meal out of an empty larder. Neither can you offer inspiring conversation out of an empty mind. Read, think, learn. Store away worthwhile tidbits that you think one friend or acquaintance might enjoy.

That doesn't mean you can't share problems. Your friend should feel honored to have your confidence. It all depends on the tone in which you talk about problems—whether positive or negative. Or whether you're actually looking for a solution, or just stirring up the rubbish.

We all want friends. They're worth any price we pay. Shakespeare in his sonnet, "Remembrance of Things Past," summons up all the sorrows and losses of the past, and then concludes:

> *But if the while I think on thee, dear friend*
> *All losses are restored and sorrows end.*

SEVEN ✿ CHILDREN—
Will They
Make You Happier?

How many troubles are with children born!
Yet he that wants them counts himself forlorn.

Sir John Scot, *Verses*

Will you be happier in your old age if you have children
than if you don't? Not according to a study of 2,583 people
50 and older by two sociologists (Norval D. Glenn, University of Texas; Sara McLanahan, University of Wiscon-
sin). Some of the people questioned had no children, some
had grown children. Overall, having children seemed to
have little effect on total happiness. Whether parents had
large families or small made no difference.

Yet the Bible says, "Children are a gift of the Lord; the
fruit of the womb is a reward. Like arrows in the hand of a
warrior, so are the children of one's youth. How blessed
[happy] is the man whose quiver is full of them" (Ps. 127:3-
5).

What's gone wrong? It looks like there are a lot of rocks out there to be avoided on the way toward enjoyment of grown children. What are they? Is it OK to let your marriage go to pot while you concentrate on your children for happiness? If you sacrifice everything for your children, won't they make it up to you?

No One Else Can Make You Happy

Don't your children owe you happiness? No. No one else can make you happy. You have to figure out how to make yourself happy. As the one who's been around longer, you should be able to help your children on that score, not by direct action but by example.

The Bible has a lot to say about happiness. And it's almost all contrary to what you'd naturally think. The Old Testament uses the Hebrew word *esher* many times. "Blessed—happy, fortunate, prosperous and enviable—is the man who . . ." (Ps. 1:1, AMP). Who what? Avoids the counsel of the ungodly, plants his life by the living water, looks to God, trusts in Him, knows Him, dwells in His house, fears Him, keeps His commandments, waits for Him. Having a quiver full of children can be a source of happiness, but not by any means the whole picture.

The New Testament uses the Greek word *makarios* many times. It means happy, fortunate, well-off. Happy are those who are poor in spirit, meek, merciful, pure in heart, persecuted for righteousness' sake, reviled for Christ. Happy are those who mourn, hunger and thirst after righteousness, grasp Jesus' teachings, serve Him faithfully, have fellowship with Him. Happiness, says the New Testament, comes with being forgiven by God. It comes with learning that giving is more satisfying than receiving. It comes with endurance of temptation and testing. It comes with reading, hearing, and heeding the Word of God, with watching for the Lord's coming. Happy even are those who die in the Lord.

Happiness, it appears, is strictly a by-product. You pursue certain worthwhile goals, fill your mind with the right thoughts. You ask God to help you shape your feelings and attitudes into what you know they ought to be. And along the way you discover—amazingly—that you're happy!

There's no hint in the Bible that happiness can ever come from manipulating other people—children, grand-children, anybody—into meeting your demands and con-forming to your wishes.

True, the aged John said, "I have no greater joy than this, to hear of my children walking in the truth" (3 John 4). He was speaking of his spiritual children, and this desire is even more true for our physical children. "Walking in the truth" means being conformed to the image of Christ, not conformed to a parent's projections for his child. "Walking in the truth" means serving Christ, which includes giving to a parent what belongs to him in that role. But only what belongs to the parent—not the child's whole life. The big-gest boulder of all in the way of parent-children relation-ships is the expectation of what a person has no right to expect. This is true for both parents and children.

You find happiness by attaching yourself to God, not to your grown child. You can enhance your comfort and hap-piness by doing everything possible for yourself. A little book by Mildred Newman and Bernard Berkowitz, *How to Be Your Own Best Friend,* has many practical suggestions on what you can do for yourself that you might expect from others. Hecato wrote in his *Fragments,* "I have begun to be a friend to myself." Seneca, the Roman philosopher, com-mented on Hecato's declaration, "That was indeed a great benefit; such a person can never be alone. You may be sure that such a man is a friend to all mankind" (Seneca, *Epis-tulae ad Lucilium,* Epis. vi, sec. 7).

Loading your children with guilt by neglecting your own well-being and happiness will not draw them to you. Psychologists call such behavior "passive manipulation." Young children frequently complain, "I have nothing to do." To voice or act out the same complaint is not appropriate behavior for parents. You've had a lifetime to learn how to keep yourself busy and happy. If you haven't learned, it's time to start. The writer of Proverbs says it's a greater victory to rule your own spirit than to conquer a city (16:32). Ruling your own spirit includes figuring out how to make yourself happy. You dare not ignore your own needs and expect your children to fulfill those needs.

Keep Your Marriage Fresh

Parents dare not neglect their marriage and look to their children. Isaac and Rebekah started out with great tenderness, as do many couples today. "Isaac brought her into his mother Sarah's tent, and he took Rebekah, and she became his wife; and he loved her; thus Isaac was comforted . . . after his mother's death" (Gen. 24:67).

However, along the way they became more involved with their children than with each other. We see them as parents of grown children plotting against each other through their children. The marriage had seriously deteriorated.

Marriage is not a solid state but a process. It's a fluid relationship that assumes many different forms throughout a lifetime. A marriage is always either growing or deteriorating.

Some studies show deterioration in up to one-third of marriages in the late years. With pressures of child-rearing and job lifted, husband and wife may face each other for 24 hours a day. Sometimes they shut themselves away from the outside world, expecting everything from each other. Inevitably they're disappointed. No single relationship can carry such a load.

They must have other relationships, other interests.

They need to spend a portion of each day apart. Otherwise, what do they have to bring to each other?

Actually, you can go apart even while sitting in the same room, if you'll give each other a chance to read or to pursue a private interest. Bart and I often spend hours on vacations utterly lost to each other even while sitting in the same little cabin or room. We're each off in our own world. But what fun it is to come together again, bubbling over with all we've separately discovered. A healthy separateness is as necessary for married people as for parents and children. It doesn't have to be geographical.

Sex can't be counted on to hold a marriage together to the end. Popular magazines are always printing bright little articles about how sex can last forever. Half the people over 65 continue to have sex, a quarter of those over 75. But that means half or three-quarters do not. Such a statistic suggests that marriage, if it's going to last, had better develop a variety of glues to hold it together. Companionship—emotional, social, intellectual, and spiritual ties—had better be ready to take over when sex falters.

Couples need to watch that bad qualities like nagging don't become exaggerated. Remember, whatever you are, you'll become more so as you get older. The Book of Proverbs has a lot to say about the contentious woman. "Better to live in a desert than with a quarrelsome and ill-tempered wife" (21:19, NIV). One man said, after he divorced his wife of 39 years, "I just wanted a few years of peace before I died."

On the other hand, the Bible gives a lovely picture of well-seasoned marriage. "Let your fountain be blessed, and rejoice in the wife of your youth, a lovely hind, a graceful doe. Let her affection fill you at all times with delight, be infatuated always with her love" (Prov. 5:18-19, RSV).

Peyton Marshall says the marriage of his grandparents, Vernon and Vidie Patterson, is still totally alive after 62 years. "They're very much tuned in to meeting each other's needs," he says. "They think ahead, plan ahead, do everything together. Vernon still writes poetry to Vidie on their wedding anniversary."

A String of Generations

What do you want to give to your children and grandchildren? What do you want from them? Any relationship is made up of giving and receiving. "Children's children are a crown to the aged"—that's what they give you. "And parents are the pride of their children"—that's what you give them (Prov. 17:6, NIV).

You can give your children pride in the way you're conducting your life—whether you're living an active life or gaining victory of spirit over a sick body. Your children want to feel good about you. Radiating an atmosphere of happiness means making the very most of every situation—whether living independently, with your children, or in a retirement or nursing home. My grandfather, a cheerful presence till he died at 91, used to say, "What can't be cured must be endured." He acted out his philosophy of making the best of things.

However, besides what the generations can give each other by being, there's also some doing required to maintain a relationship. To what extent should you work at family harmony?

With larger families and a shorter life span, the relationship of the generations used to be like a pyramid. Many younger people supported a very few old people. Now the generations relate more like a string of beads, with maybe a double or triple strand in some spots but, nevertheless, a string. Job, who suffered so much, was finally depicted in the Bible as enjoying the ultimate blessing: "And after this Job lived 140 years, and saw his sons, and his grandsons, four generations" (Job 42:16).

Today, it's not unusual to see four generations. On Mother's Day and Father's Day, Bart asks for great-great-grandparents to stand, then great-grandparents, and so on, down to parents. Out of 2,500 people in attendance at three services, there will be maybe one or two great-great-grandmothers or fathers. That's five generations. In every service there will be half a dozen great-grandparents—four generations. A host will stand up as grandparents, and more as parents.

Today, there's nothing unusual about becoming a grandparent. You can't decide that grandparenthood means it's time to sit back and "let the younger folks carry the load." There aren't enough of them anymore. We all have to carry our share of the load. "Bear one another's burdens, and thus fulfill the law of Christ" (Gal. 6:2). Whoever's strong at the time, whether old or young, must help the other.

An older generation needs to be careful about laying impossible burdens on the middle generation. People in their 40s and 50s may be carrying both parents and children, sometimes even aged grandparents plus their own grandchildren. They may feel squeezed financially, trapped in a line of work they'd like to get out of, pressed emotionally.

In many ways, little and big, parents can make the load less heavy for their adult children. Anything they do for their grandchildren will help. My mother didn't have a lot of strength to do big things, but I used to think it was such a help the way she'd come and just talk to the children. She'd pick up a napkin they had dropped and explain how it should be folded neatly. All sorts of little things like that. Children have so very many things to learn.

Contacts between generations typically involve an elaborate exchange of goods and services which flow from parent to child about as often as from adult child to parent. Each person in this string of generations needs to keep alert to what he can contribute to the ongoing family relationship. Each may become a resource in emergencies. "A friend loves at all times, and a brother is born for adversity" (Prov. 17:17). Each one contributes love, encouragement, support.

Contacts are maintained by visits, phone calls, letters, errands, gifts. Sometimes families go to the same church or club. Sometimes several generations of people enjoy small shared trips, or a vacation together. Our sons go camping together. We have had some delightful seashore and mountain vacations with our daughter Deborah and family, who live the farthest away. We've taken several extended trips with our daughter Janet.

Adult Children

A relationship with adult children must be fluid. When your children were young, you trained them for independence. The more you succeeded in helping them to be independent, the more completely you'll have them back now as adult friends. They won't have to fight you for their freedom, or stay away from you to find their own identity. The relationship keeps changing as children and parents develop different needs.

The most direct way to become aware of changes in people is to listen. One grandmother, Dr. Elizabeth Holmes, a retired school principal, told me, "I've set as a goal to be a better listener. I mean really listen—for the feelings behind the words. Each day I ask the Lord to help me, and each day I confess to Him when I think I've failed. I tend to overwhelm my family with too much talking, too much knowing how everything should be done."

It's by listening, by sharing our own feelings, by interacting with those we love, that we can keep a relationship flexible and growing. Preserving a relationship is more important than being right about everything.

If we think of our grown children as friends, we won't order them about, or demand that they do certain things for us. "Oh, it is excellent to have a giant's strength; but it is tyrannous to use it like a giant" (Shakespeare). We won't presume on our position as parents. We'll politely request, or we'll appeal if we have a real need. We'll respect the time of our grown children as much as we respect the time of our friends.

Living Together

In the vast majority of cases, parents and grown children prefer to live separately. Only one over-65 person in ten is unable to be totally independent.

Special problems present themselves when families must double up. Sometimes young adults or young families move in with parents because of some emergency—loss of job, divorce, illness. Or it may be the other way around—parents move in with their children. The problems of relationship are intensified by closeness.

When children live with parents, or parents with children, it's essential to work out territorial rights and areas of responsibility and time. If you divide up responsibility for meal preparation, for example, and agree on general guidelines, each should have complete independence to spend the grocery money and prepare the food in his or her own way.

Those needing privacy should be able to go into their own rooms and count on not being disturbed. If Grandmother lives in the home, she should have one room or space which she can arrange or furnish her own way. It's all part of respecting each other's individuality, not submerging another personality in one's own atmosphere. No person can demand that everything suit him. If the house seems too cool to an older person, he can wear thermal underwear, or put his feet on a heating pad.

One family in our church has four generations living under the same roof—and radiating love, joy, peace in the process. It can be done.

Grandchildren

If you don't have grandchildren of your own, you can adopt some. Gertrude Rutgers has never married, but she has a closer relationship with her nephews and nieces than many people have with their own children. Gertrude, who is 92, says, "My nephew and niece are so devoted they come to get me every Sunday after church, and drive me back to my apartment after eating dinner and spending the afternoon together. That is, if the weather is bad and I can't drive myself. I'm independent—I can take care of myself. I'm strong enough to do all I need to do for myself. But I know I've got someone to depend on. When I broke my kneecap, someone called them from the hospital, and my niece was there immediately. They kept me in their home for seven weeks and urged me to stay longer. They tell me that whenever I can't manage my apartment, I can live with them. They always remember my birthday and Christmas. I keep up a correspondence with the nephews and nieces who live at a distance.

"Sometimes I wonder if I can ever be grateful enough for my blessings. I thank God every day, just constantly. But it's almost impossible to appreciate enough all the blessings I have."

I asked Gertrude what she had done to make her nephews and nieces so fond of her.

She replied, "I suppose it's because I did so much for them when they were little, loved them so much. I spent time with them as children—took them out, did things with them. Just loved them a lot. I felt they needed an extra amount of love because they knew they were adopted."

Peyton Marshall has a wonderful picture of the Pattersons as grandparents. "They were very involved with all their grandchildren. They lived two hours away, but were always there for all birthdays and special occasions. Or there'd be a phone call, card, present. When we stayed at their house, we would be "invited" to take part in their morning devotions. Or they'd stay at our home over a weekend while our parents went away. They were very strong, very firm people. Grandpa was no pushover—he would spank just as Dad would. They still keep up correspondence with all the grandchildren, and now even include the spouses of the grandchildren and the great-grandchildren. I had them on a pedestal as a child."

It's very important to me to try to be a good grandmother. I've had a three-month-old baby in my home when I had to go out and teach Bible classes. My daughter-in-law had strep throat and a high fever, and my son wanted to get the baby out of the house before he caught the germ. I said, "Of course. I'll just get a baby-sitter when I have to be gone." I loved it.

I've taken a one-week leave of absence from my classes to care for three little boys in Grand Rapids while their mother went to the hospital to have a fourth. Cheri said she was able to enjoy her hospital stay knowing that the children were in good hands.

I flew to New Jersey to be with our daughter Deborah for a week when she had a new baby, had to get ready to move in two weeks, and her husband needed to be in the Netherlands for his sister's wedding. I've picked up children at nursery school, baby-sat when I could. Though I'm not really a superduty, full-time grandma, still I very much enjoy doing what I can. Especially I like to talk with the grandchildren. I enjoy their little quirks of mind. They're growing up so fast. I don't want to look back and feel I've lost an opportunity.

If you don't work at relationships, you won't have them. "Can two walk together, except they make an appointment and have agreed?" (Amos 3:3, AMP) You have to reach out to each other enough to understand. You have to agree on what is enough and what is too much.

I used to think that a proper mother of young adult children wrote a letter every week to each child. My mother had always kept in touch that way. So, very efficiently, I typed off copies of a general letter and then wrote a personal note to each. Not very many letters came back, but I wrote anyway—I was doing my part, I thought. But word came to me from a daughter-in-law via my daughter that she didn't like receiving those letters—they only made her feel guilty about not answering them.

So, I heaved a sigh of relief, and adopted the modern way—I call up when I feel like it. They call as often as we do, sometimes every day in times of crisis, other times not for a month. Nobody feels guilty, and we really enjoy each other—as friends.

If the cost of the telephone call looms large to the son or daughter, it's understood that they're to call when they feel like talking—in the discount hours, of course. Then we'll ask them to hang up, and we'll call back. When I'm talking half an hour or an hour on a long distance call, I sometimes say, "Think of all the money I'm saving over flying to see you." This is a little luxury that we enjoy. Since we no longer have to pay for children's shoes, or music lessons, or orthodontics, the few dollars for phone calls don't seem excessive.

To our fellow grandparents, Bart and I say to stay independent as long as possible. Keep your family relationships as a two-way street. If the time comes when your children must care for you, respond gratefully.

You can't change your grown children. But you can change yourself to improve a relationship.

EIGHT 🌿:
MONEY–
What Can You Do
About It?

There is no dignity quite so impressive, and no independence quite so important, as living within your means.

Calvin Coolidge

Is money your good servant, on hand when you need it? Or is it a slave driver, jabbing at you with terrifying force?

Is there a right or wrong way to handle money? Most of us carry attitudes toward money which were formed by our early experiences.

The spring before I was due to go off to college, my father took a 40 percent cut in his modest salary as a minister. The Depression had hit our middle-class community in Chicago with its full fury. I heard my parents talk about people out of work, about investments that had gone bad. My brother and I went to college anyway. Our parents cut into their food budget and used up savings accounts to send us. Money I'd put aside for clothes went for tuition. My childhood savings "for college" were immediately utilized. You can be sure my brother and I didn't waste very much of our one-dollar-a-week allowances.

Young people have grown up in an expanding economy, with its inflationary psychology. If you didn't spend now, the price would only go higher. Money saved would be worthless later on. If you borrowed you'd be paying back in cheaper dollars. So the limit on credit was whatever you could get.

When that era ended, debts came due which couldn't be paid. People lost farms, businesses, houses, investment properties. Many went into bankruptcy, utterly mystified as to why their faith in the future didn't pay off.

Different generations have differing attitudes toward money, says an article in the *Wall Street Journal.* It describes a three-generation family in Cincinnati, Ohio. Grandma, 85, learned from the Depression that income and assets could disappear. She's afraid of credit cards and any form of debt. Her main concern is holding onto what she has.

Her son, 59, experienced a hard childhood, developed a compelling desire to succeed. He's been interested in making money through work and investments, in saving and building.

Her grandson, 27, has known only affluence, and mostly spends. The only saving he manages is "enforced saving," buying a house and paying for insurance.

The grandmother feels the enormous difference in viewpoint of the generations. "Our grandchildren are like everybody's grandchildren. When they want anything, they get it."

Is there a standard for handling money? If your conditioning has been wrong, can you correct it?

The Bible has a lot to say about money. It tells us how to keep from being so poor that we're tortured by lack. It also tells us not to be greedy.

Give me neither poverty nor riches; feed me with the food that is my portion, lest I be full and deny Thee and say, "Who is the Lord?" Or lest I be in want and steal, and profane the name of my God (Prov. 30:8-9).

Managing Your Money

That all elderly people are poor is one of those myths of old age. Wealth or poverty cannot be defined by dollars alone. There is also the matter of your skill in handling money, as well as the way you perceive yourself. A Harris survey asked if lack of money was a problem for those over 65. Of those *under* 65, about 68 percent thought it a "very serious" problem. In contrast only 17 percent of those over 65 found it so. A study done by the National Council on Aging showed that of those who are poor in old age, a high proportion have always been relatively poor.

Having "enough" money is a matter of bringing income and outgo together. That's why you can't draw an arbitrary line. Some people are better at stretching money than others. They garden, sew, can, freeze, repair cars, build onto their houses, and hunt bargains. A serious gap between income and outgo can occur even with a high income. When people confuse desires with needs, they will think they don't have enough money, no matter what the amount.

The biblical ideal is to handle money in such a way as to be free—free to live the Christian life without worry. Christ said that when a person is overly taken up with money, whether he has little or much, his life is like thorny ground. The seed of the Word, if sown there, will be choked out and produce nothing. "And the one on whom seed was sown among the thorns, this is the man who hears the Word, and the worry of the world, and the deceitfulness of riches choke the Word, and it becomes unfruitful" (Matt. 13:22). So either not enough or too much can produce the same effect.

The Apostle Paul wrote, "Owe nothing to anyone except to love one another," (Rom. 13:8). The principle may sound extreme to some, but Bart and I have followed it. We think it's a pretty comfortable way to live. We've never been approached by a bill collector, never feared unwelcome phone calls or letters or telegrams. We've never worried that something might be repossessed to rob us of equity already paid for. We've never paid the high interest rates required by installment or credit buying.

Like Paul, we "know how to get along with humble means" (Phil. 4:12). We didn't own a car till we'd been married nine years and had four children. We walked, Bart used public transportation for his calls, or someone drove us. We borrowed from my parents toward our first car, after that, however difficult it was, we saved up before buying and paid cash for each car.

Some studies have shown that finances can be an important contributing factor to marital distress, even leading to divorce. We never had any stress over money. When we didn't have money, we didn't spend.

How did we ever arrive at this pay-as-you-go basis? I can assure you it didn't come naturally. We received some good advice when we were young. On returning from our honeymoon, we were all set to go to Marshall Field's in Chicago and pick out some furniture which we felt expressed our tastes. We had already decided on the style—18th-century mahogany. But we hadn't thought about how we would pay for the furniture.

Bart's mother tactfully pointed out to us that if we hoped to take that trip to Europe we were talking about, we'd better not be tied up in heavy payments for furniture. She thought a trip to Europe on our income was an even wilder idea than buying good furniture, but she knew how to appeal to us. She suggested buying secondhand furniture and paying cash as we went along. Bart's father helped us run down bargains. We furnished our first apartment that way—no rug on the floor until we could afford it. But we were financially solvent.

After a year or so, we picked out an expensive three-month tour of Europe, and tried to float a loan from my parents. My mother pointed out that we hadn't saved anything yet, but said that as soon as we had saved half of what we needed, they would loan us the other half. In the course of saving that half, by means of stringent economies, we learned what money was. We also figured out how we could manage the grand tour of Europe for about half what we first thought it would cost.

We've always felt that Bart's mother taught us how to spend money, and my mother taught us how to save. After those first three years, we could make money do what we wanted it to.

Later, when we had four children in college and graduate school at the same time, a man in our church said, "I don't know how in the world you do what you are doing on your income." He knew it wasn't large. Around that time one of our daughters said to us, "You know, you people really live beyond your income. I mean, you travel, you dress well, you spend for music lessons, education." That was the stage of life when we had one car and six drivers in the family! We bought good clothes secondhand. We had long before acquired fine furniture secondhand. We never ever went out to restaurants. We ate whatever happened to be on sale in the meat or produce sections at the supermarket.

We all have our pet economies and extravagances. There isn't much logic in these choices since they are matters of individual taste. Yet it is the little or big extravagances that make the economies endurable.

Like Paul, we also learned how to live in prosperity (Phil. 4:12). It feels like luxury to me not to have to add up my purchases before approaching a checkout counter. I'm profoundly thankful to be free from time-consuming economies. It means more time for writing and speaking. But economies never interfered with our happiness—we have always had peace of mind. At some stages of life people have more money than time or energy, and at other stages more time than money. Either can be substituted quite effectively for the other.

"Use it up, wear it out, make it do, or do without." To our way of thinking, a little discipline in spending is a lot pleasanter than worrying about debts and bill collectors. There is evidence that Americans act on this principle when they have to—trash and garbage tonnage decrease considerably in an economic slump.

The Bible also tells us to earn money in order to avoid poverty. In our day of compulsory retirement, you'll feel better equipped for old age if you think about some means of earning money after retirement. Since many people working full-time have more money than time, service functions are in great demand. Many retirees earn extra money by handyman work, tutoring, teaching, office work, part-time janitor service, baby-sitting, house-sitting, part-time nursing.

A young man in our neighborhood was out of work for a while. He picked up extra money by selling old newspapers which he gathered from the neighbors, and by doing odd jobs. Bart and I were delighted to let him clean our cars, and gratefully paid him three times the auto-wash price. We didn't have time to do the polishing, but liked having it done.

A retiree who lives across the street from our lawyer son takes care of Dan's yard along with his own. It's beautiful! "Make it your ambition to lead a quiet life, to mind your own business and to work with your hands . . . so that your daily life may win the respect of outsiders and so that you will not be dependent on anybody" (1 Thes. 4:11-12, NIV).

Avoid Greed

Besides avoiding poverty, the Bible also tells us to avoid greed. "Do not weary yourself to gain wealth, cease from your consideration of it. When you set your eyes on it, it is gone. For wealth certainly makes itself wings, like an eagle that flies toward the heavens" (Prov. 23:4-5). The last of the Ten Commandments warns us not to covet (Ex. 20:17). People who have everything this world can offer may discover they still experience a strange restlessness, a hunger. Somehow we're created with a dimension that simply cannot be satisfied with material goods, however fine they are. Jesus said, "Beware, and be on your guard against every form of greed; for not even when one has an abundance does his life consist of his possessions" (Luke 12:15). This longing for something beyond the immediate is an intimation of our immortality. We're created for eternity and we need to see our possessions in that perspective.

The preacher in Ecclesiastes, viewing life from the point of view of the natural man, said, "He who loves money will not be satisfied with money, nor will he who loves abundance with its income . . . When good things increase, those who consume them increase" (Ecc. 5:10-11). The more you own, the more you have to take care of, whether it's silver, knickknacks, a boat or summer home, or investments. There's a restfulness about simplicity of living. I just don't want too much stuff around me. Enough is enough. I love to unload by giving away.

Wise Use of Money

How do you arrive at that happy median between poverty and greed? To avoid poverty in old age, you need to save. Saving is deferred gratification, and needs to be learned early. Old age income, whether Social Security, pension, or private savings, means that consumption during one's work life is curtailed in return for consumption during retirement. Some people think that because Social Security and pension are taken out of their paychecks, they don't need to save. But Social Security was never intended to be enough to live on. It was intended to supplement private pensions and personal savings.

For many people, retirement means a painful drop in income. The tragedy about pensions is that millions of workers contributing to pension plans never collect a cent in benefits. A Senate investigator said the rate of noncollection is as high as 9 out of 10 in some industries. A worker can't carry his pension with him from one job to another if it's not "vested." The pension system may not be insured against bad investments or bankruptcy. The worker may be laid off before retirement age. The amount may be eaten away by inflation. There may be no survivor's benefits. Many small and large companies have simply gone out of business and their pension funds went with them. So check on your pension fund.

Americans typically find it hard to save in a credit-card economy. We have an extremely low savings rate compared with other countries (5.7 percent of take-home pay compared to 18.7 percent in Japan). For society as a whole, that means not enough money available for families to borrow for houses, and for businesses to borrow for improved means of production. For the individual—because of early retirement and increased longevity—it means not enough money in old age. A man at 65 can figure on an average of 14 years of life, a woman on 18 years.

Social Security plus pension may not prove sufficient to maintain the standard of living to which you have become accustomed. So you need investments. In Old Testament times, wealth grew primarily in flocks and herds. The writer of Proverbs said, "Know well the condition of your flocks, and pay attention to your herds; for riches are not forever" (Prov. 27:23-24).

The modern way of saving is in banks, stocks, bonds, or real estate. It's a good idea to read a few good books on general principles of investing. Know where to put your money so it will yield the income you need. A few basic principles stand out:

■ Spread the risk. Don't put it all into one company, bank, or insurance plan. Money can take wings. No investment is without risk.

■ Always figure the downside risk. Could I survive if I lost this particular investment?

■ What kinds of investment am I comfortable with? The objective is peace of mind, freedom from worry. Some like more speculative investments than others. Pick what suits your personality, whether an income property added onto your house, an account in a savings and loan association, stocks, bonds, or a bank account. People have differing ideas of how much effort they want to put into investments. Some want to work with their hands, taking care of a building that produces rent. Others want to work with figures on paper. Some prefer mutual funds or insurance, handing over the responsibility to someone else.

Watch Out for Fraud

Wise handling of money involves watching out for fraud. Many frauds are aimed at older people. Older people don't automatically lose their intelligence and judgment, but they do become more vulnerable because of special wants or hopes. It's a good idea to start well ahead of time to become informed about varying types of quackery. The appeal is often based on powerful psychological needs or desires.

A widow was sold a condominium she thought she could afford. After the purchase, she learned that she had to pay a huge monthly maintenance fee which could go up at any time. A retired college teacher spent $20,000 on a franchise for fruit juice vending machines. He wasn't told that in his territory vandals would destroy the machines regularly, or that people wouldn't buy enough juice to pay for his investment, let alone give him any profit. He finally wrote it off as a loss.

It's probably a good thing to be cheated a few times early in life. "Money is never spent to so much advantage as when you have been cheated out of it: for at one stroke you have purchased prudence" (Arthur Schopenhauer, *Aphorisms: Wisdom of Life*).

All kinds of frauds appeal to older people who can least afford loss: anti-aging schemes—lotions, mechanical devices, exercise salons that go out of business. Get-rich-quick schemes. Quack remedies. Real estate at a distance, bogus home improvements, dishonest auto repairs. Work-at-home schemes like stuffing envelopes, or making something for which you have to pay a fee in advance for materials. Insurance as a supplement to Medicare or group coverage—with fine print that excludes practically everything. Schemes for getting money out of your bank account.

In addition to public fraud, there is private fraud in families or between friends.

> I once had Money and a Friend;
>   Of either, thought I store.
> I lent my Money to my Friend
>   And took his word therefore.
> I sought my Money from my Friend.
>   Which I had wanted long,
> I lost my Money and my Friend;
>   Now was not that a wrong?
>   (Unknown)

If your children want to borrow money, of course you want to help them. Paul wrote to the Corinthians, "Here for this third time I am ready to come to you, and I will not be a burden to you; for I do not seek what is yours, but you; for children are not responsible to save up for their parents, but parents for their children" (2 Cor. 12:14).

We all love to give gifts to our children. But don't give them your security, with the expectation that they can take care of you later on. They may want to and not be able to.

When it comes to lending, let grown children establish their own credit. And *don't lend them more than you can get along without*. After all, if they can't pay, you know you're not going to gouge them to get back what they owe. So be careful about lending. Disappointment, bitterness, pressure, and guilt don't improve relationships.

Giving
There's one investment which won't go bad, and that is giving to God's work. The Bible regards giving as basic to wise handling of money.

> Do not lay up for yourselves treasures upon earth, where moth and rust destroy, and where thieves break in and steal. But lay up for yourselves treasures in heaven, where neither moth nor rust destroys, and where thieves do not break in or steal; for where your treasure is, there will your heart be also (Matt. 6:19-21).

Some people live simply to give generously to the Lord's work and to the poor. The Bible says that giving affords us a security beyond insurance. "Give, and it will be given to you" (Luke 6:38). This is true in human relations, and it's true of God. Giving is a place where we can interact with God. Bart and I have always given one-tenth of our gross income to God's work, no matter how tight the money. The tithe came out first, *not* last after all bills were paid. We just never figured that that one-tenth was ours. And our needs were always provided for. Neither we nor our children came out with debts for their education. A serious illness of one child fell between the cracks of insurance policies and wasn't covered. It required thousands of dollars for treatment, but somehow money came in to pay the bills. We never suffered from lack of money, nor had to borrow. The Lord does provide, and He piles up many other benefits as well.

By now God has provided us with enough to cushion our lives in various ways. We can afford some help and we're able to travel with more comfort. We are free to do His work. It is a serious mistake to be stingy with God. Luke's words about giving continue: "A good measure, pressed down, shaken together and running over, will be poured into your lap. For with the measure you use, it will be measured to you" (6:38, NIV).

Now, we don't think a tithe is nearly enough to give to God's work. It doesn't begin to feel like giving until we've gone beyond the tenth.

Enjoy Your Money

After you've worked, saved, invested wisely, given—enjoy your money. "Godliness with contentment is great gain. For we brought nothing into the world, and we can take nothing out of it. But if we have food and clothing, we will be content with that" (1 Tim. 6:6-8, NIV).

Love, joy, and peace can make a delight out of very little. "Better a little with the fear of the Lord than great wealth with turmoil" (Prov. 15:16, NIV). The emotional atmosphere of the home matters far more in the enjoyment of a meal than the menu. "Better is a dish of vegetables where love is, than a fattened ox and hatred with it"

(Prov. 15:17).

"God . . . richly supplies us with all things to enjoy" (1 Tim. 6:17). As long as we're in this world, we're to accept and enjoy the good gifts God gives us, and to follow His common sense measures for handling our resources.

Elmer and Elsie Hubler lived a beautiful life of service to God on a very limited income. Elsie said one time, "I knew the promise, 'My God shall supply all your needs according to His riches in glory in Christ Jesus' (Phil. 4:19). But I still worried. We just didn't have any extra money at all. When our old washing machine broke down completely, I didn't know how we'd ever get another one. But in a few days, from a totally unexpected source, a check came through the mail for the exact amount that we needed for a new washer. After that I never again worried about money. I knew by experience that God really would provide."

God has given us intelligence and instruction in the Bible as to how to handle money. He expects us to use both of those to plan ahead. Yet when plans go wrong, beyond our mistakes and disappointments, God is the real source for our needs. Essentially we have to trust Him.

NINE ❧:
NUTRITION—
Who's in Charge
of Your Health?

May you live all the days of your life.

Jonathan Swift

Overheard in a doctor's waiting room: "If I'd known I was going to live so long, I'd have taken better care of myself."

When you reach 65 years of age, you face an average of 16 to 17 more years of life. Do you want to spend those years with a collection of ailments—or in the best health possible you can have? To a large extent, you choose the degree of health you want.

I asked Dr. Paul Parker what problem he ran into most constantly in his medical practice.

Without hesitation he answered, "Lifestyle. There are 11 diseases that people bring on themselves by the way they live: hypertension, heart attack, strokes, diabetes, lung cancer, cancer of the intestine, gall stones, hiatus hernia, diverticulosis, cirrhosis, hemorrhoids. And their prevention is so simple. But people find it very, very hard to change their habits. They want a pill or a treatment or even bypass heart surgery before they'll recast their habits."

You don't build a new pattern of living all at once when you find out you need bypass heart surgery. But you can begin building habits right now that make for long and successful life. The same habits may even keep you from needing bypass heart surgery, says Dr. Parker.

Maggie Lettvin is a proponent of physical fitness in the Boston area. Through books, TV programs, and movies, she inspires other people to keep or get in shape by exercise and diet. She's married to Jerome Lettvin, M.D., Professor of Medicine at Massachusetts Institute of Technology, who weighs 300 pounds and smokes four packages of cigarettes a day. She says of her husband, "He is utterly brilliant, utterly charming, and utterly self-indulgent, and I love him just the way he is. . . . I only present options for people who are looking for optimal health. Not everybody is looking for that."

Are you? Every inch that you move toward sound health practices will improve your health. What degree of health are you willing to settle for?

It never ceases to amaze me how much trouble people will take to stay alive or cope with ills once they have them. They'll take drugs with bad side effects, set their alarms to take pills around the clock, undergo surgery, struggle with walkers and prosthetic devices, make wearisome trips to the doctor's office for shots or treatments. They'll even follow stringent diets to cope with heart trouble or high blood pressure. Why couldn't they summon up the same willpower to prevent those diseases from developing? The body is a delicate and valuable machine which requires certain procedures for maintenance.

Gertrude Rutgers, 92, says with spirit, "I firmly believe that more than half of the old people who are invalids have made themselves invalids. They won't follow orders, they won't do what they have to do to be well. I've had various problems which I have overcome. After Mother and Dad died, and my sister died, I was alone. I did no real cooking for myself for a long time, and I got diverticulitis. When the doctor questioned me as to the cause, he said coffee was bad for this. He also said irregularity of meals could cause it and that I was to have three meals a day at regular times. I followed instructions. Now I cook for myself and eat regularly. I got over the diverticulitis."

Nutrition researchers tell us that what we will be in 10, 20, and 30 years depends on the food choices we make now. Preparation for good health in later years must begin before they arrive—preferably in infancy. Every day you live, you're either building or tearing down your health.

Health, when you have it, is like air or water. You appreciate it only when it's gone. Gerontologists, nutritionists, and physical fitness experts not only want us to add years to our lives. Even more important, they want us to add life to our years.

The Bible and Your Body
The aged John wrote to believers, "Beloved, I pray that in all respects you may prosper and be in good health, just as your soul prospers" (3 John 2). Christ incarnated Himself in a body. The Gospels describe the way He lived among His people. Children were attracted to Him, He held them in His arms. He must have had an attractive physical body.

The Christian faith puts major emphasis upon the resurrection of Christ's body. After His resurrection, He ate, He cooked, He broke bread. He was no phantom. The body was the vehicle of His existence in this world. "The Word became flesh, and dwelt among us" (John 1:14).

The body is the vehicle of our existence. Care of and reverence for the body is essential to becoming a fully functioning person.

> Do you not know that your body is a temple of the
> Holy Spirit who is in you, whom you have from God,
> and that you are not your own? For you have been
> bought with a price; therefore glorify God in your body
> (1 Cor. 6:19-20).

Your body is your instrument for giving and receiving
love—in marriage, in family relations, with friends. Because you meet other people's needs through your body, the
care you give it is not merely selfish.

Christ showed concern for the body when He healed the
sick, fed the 5,000, served breakfast to the disciples. He
said, "I came that they might have life, and might have it
abundantly" (John 10:10). A healthy body is certainly part
of living abundantly. God the Creator starts most of us off
with the potential for a healthy body. Whether we realize
that potential or not is pretty much up to us.

Body Maintenance

It's part of the stereotype that to be old is to be sick and to
look pale and withered. The fact is that to be young is to be
sick sometimes, to be middle-aged is to be sick sometimes,
and to be old is to be sick sometimes. Too many doctors and
patients alike confuse sickness with old age. If a doctor says,
"What can you expect at your age?" consult another doctor. Disease at any age is something you can fight.

A doctor one time told me that I was probably suffering
from allergies, but at my age there was no use going to an
allergist. I might spend a lot of money and get no results.
Eventually I went to an allergist who said, "At your age we
can expect results seven out of ten times." I determined to
be one of the seven. I went for the shots faithfully, gave
myself every boost possible with rest, exercise, and diet,

and got 100 percent results. No more asthma or swollen sinuses. Asthma runs in my family. But I'm willing to fight for health.

The amount of care and attention required to keep the old chassis running increases with age. In my opinion it's worth any amount of trouble to feel good. Efforts to build or maintain health don't distract me nearly as much from what I want to do as sickness would.

I love to look at well-disciplined, healthy bodies of any age. A good skin, bright eyes, healthy hair, and a stream-lined body come along as by-products when you eat well to feel good.

In business there is a lot of talk about the principle of entropy—the tendency of all life to disintegrate, whether organic or human organization. Businesses, churches, social groups of all kinds require constant attention to keep them functioning. A house will fall to pieces if you simply stop repairing it. Webster says entropy is "the degradation of the matter and energy in the universe to an ultimate state of inert uniformity." Your body will go down hill year after year if you don't struggle to reverse or at least slow down the trend. "Inert uniformity" perfectly describes what we all fear most about old age. After death, the body gradually reverts to dust. But God offers life, growth, eternity.

> *Change and decay in all around I see*
> *O Thou who changest not, abide with me.*
> (Henry F. Lyte)

Possibilities

What are the real possibilities for an active, healthy old age? Remember, old people are not a homogeneous group. Physically, older individuals differ more widely from the mean that people of any other age group. Biological aging begins at different ages and develops at different rates. It even varies from one body organ to another. We all have our inherited tendencies toward heart, lung, stomach, or intestinal problems. By special care and treatment, we can keep the whole ship from sinking just because one panel has come loose.

What do we aim at in our health? "You will come to the grave in full vigor, like sheaves gathered in season" (Job 5:26, NIV). We all want to be healthy up to the end, then go all of a sudden. Moses achieved this. "Although Moses was 120 years old when he died, his eye was not dim, nor his vigor abated" (Deut. 34:7).

That same age—120—is mentioned in Genesis as a normal life span. "Then the Lord said, 'My Spirit shall not strive with man forever, because he also is flesh; nevertheless his days shall be 120 years" (Gen. 6:3). Modern research suggests that if the degenerative diseases can be conquered a life span of 110 or 120 is possible for modern man.

Isaiah describes conditions of life in that ideal time of the "new heavens and a new earth." "No longer will there be in it an infant who lives but a few days, or an old man who does not live out his days; for the youth will die at the age of 100 and the one who does not reach the age of 100 shall be thought accursed" (Isa. 65:20).

Scientists tell us now that such a day is within sight. Today we have 32,000 people in the United States 100 years of age and over. And some societies have 11 times as great a percentage. We keep discovering vigorous individuals in our midst who are in their 70s, 80s, or 90s. Scientists tell us how to increase life expectancy greatly by dietary manipulation. Common observation tells us that many people of 65 have about the same level of health that people of 45 used to have.

The major killers in the U.S. today are heart disease, cancer, stroke, accidents, lung disease, pneumonia and influenza, diabetes, liver disease and cirrhosis, hardening of the arteries, and suicide. All but accidents, lung disease, pneumonia and influenza, and suicide are directly attributable to diet. People used to die almost entirely from accidents or infectious diseases. Wiping out those diseases is what has increased average life expectancy so dramatically. Cutting down on degenerative diseases could further dramatically increase life expectancy.

Dr. Paul Parker says, "The medical professional formerly took little interest in nutrition, because it had not been scientifically proven that diet made a difference. Now, however, the evidence is pouring in. We cannot ignore it."

According to Frances Moore Lappe (*Diet for a Small Planet*) and others, we've made some shocking changes in our diet in the last 100 years. An 1876 issue of *Scientific American*, reporting causes of death in New York City, doesn't list a single case of cancer. Today, one person out of four will suffer from cancer and two-thirds of those will die. Likewise, it was only from 1890 on that coronary thrombosis began to appear in America. The symptoms were so unusual that nobody knew what it was. Doctors came from England to study this strange new disease. At about this time, the agonies of arthritis began to attack people.

All this happened within a 10- to 20-year period after millers began stripping flour of wheat germ. About the same time, white sugar became readily available to the masses. The era of degenerative diseases had begun.

Lappe points out the changes in our diet which have contributed to the development of degenerative disease.

■ We get most of our protein from animals instead of plants. We overlook the possibilities of beans, especially soy beans, wheat germ, and many other vegetables as low-cholesterol sources of protein.

■ We get too many of our calories in fats—42 percent. We'd be better off to cut back to 30 percent or less. This great amount of fat comes from various sources. We're eating two or three times as much meat, poultry, cheese, and margarine as we did in the mid-1940s. And it's the meat marbleized with fat that is considered choice. Many snack foods are drenched in fat. The calories in potato chips are 63 percent fat. In prepared foods such as TV dinners and in fast foods, we are consuming about half our calories in fats.

■ We eat too much sugar. Consumption has doubled since 1900, gone up 25 percent since 1960. We're overloaded with sugar in canned or frozen fruits, in canned vegetables, soft drinks, cereals, and baked goods. The second most popular breakfast cereal is half sugar in content. A 12-ounce can of soft drink contains six to nine teaspoons of sugar. Sugar is empty calories, without body-building vitamins and minerals.

■ We eat too much salt—two to ten times what the body requires. Too much salt increases the risk of heart attack and stroke, as well as kidney troubles. Fast food and processed foods come loaded with salt. Processed cheeses have six times as much salt as natural cheese. Lunch meats, cured meats, and snack foods are heavily salted. Even sweet things like a piece of chocolate cake made from a cake mix contains as much salt as does a 24-ounce bag of potato chips.

■ We eat too little fiber, and incur the risks of bowel cancer and other intestinal diseases. We need more fresh fruits and vegetables, as many eaten raw or as close to raw as possible. Cooked at home, these can be unsalted, unsweetened, not drenched in fat. Certainly the salad bars in restaurants are a big step in the right direction. Whole cereals, fruits, and vegetables should form the bulk of our diets. Legumes (peas, beans, lentils) are not only good sources of protein but also excellent sources of fiber. Doctors and nutritionists highly recommend wheat bran every day for adding fiber to the diet.

Things to Avoid

Just as we wouldn't put sand in our gas tanks, so we need to avoid putting certain things into our bodies. Because a thing grows on the earth doesn't mean it's suitable to eat or drink or smoke. God told Adam that he could eat from any tree in the garden except one (Gen. 2:16-17). Likewise, there are some things which we're not to take into our bodies.

We all know about the dangers of cigarette smoking. Also too much alcohol causes serious damage. "Do not get drunk with wine, for that is dissipation, but be filled with the Spirit" (Eph. 5:18). The Bible warns repeatedly against drunkenness. In the Old Testament the Nazarites, those specially set apart for God, gave up wine entirely. Nutritionists tell us that any at all is useless—it's empty calories.

Watch out for pollutants. Read labels in the grocery store and watch for chemical additives, as well as for salt and sugar added where least expected and needed. Eat fresh things rather than canned or processed.

Of course, avoid too many calories. Overweight causes and aggravates many degenerative diseases, including diabetes.

"Whether, then, you eat or drink or whatever you do, do all to the glory of God" (1 Cor. 10:31). Keep your refrigerator stocked with the good things to munch on, and "make no provision for the flesh in regard to its lusts" (Rom. 13:14). If possible, avoid having candy and salty snack foods at hand.

Motivating Yourself

To change your pattern of eating is difficult. I started back in my college days. I'd gained 20 pounds as a freshman and wanted to take them off. A friend gave me a book on nutrition from which I learned that I could cut my calorie count way down by simply leaving out candy and desserts entirely.

Though I still ate potatoes and the delicious whole wheat bread served in the dormitory, I shed those 20 pounds in three months. It was then I discovered I'd lost my taste for sweets! After that, one bite of dessert satisfied me—it tasted sickeningly sweet.

The next step forward came 25 years later, after some years of ill health. My basic trouble had at last been diagnosed as hypoglycemia, and I was on a high-protein, frequent-meal diet. I wanted desperately to accompany Bart on a three-month preaching and teaching mission to the Philippines, but I knew I wasn't up to it. At that time my sister gave me a book on nutrition. I read the book four times, trying to figure out how to incorporate the author's ideas into my patterns of shopping and eating and cooking. The big thing I learned from that book was the different forms proteins can take—wheat germ, nutritional yeast, dry skim milk, eggs, vegetables. I wanted variety in my high-protein diet.

I also learned about B-vitamins. Since we strip the wheat germ from our flour, and eat only a small amount of bread anyway, Americans are woefully deficient in B-vitamins. I began loading in nutritional yeast. We began eating wheat germ instead of cereal for breakfast. It's really good with raisins, dried apricots, berries, or bananas. Bart followed along in all my frantic gropings for better health. He had always had good health, but in his 40s he was beginning to feel he should slow down. For the first time, house and hospital calls seemed difficult for him.

With all those B-vitamins plus a good diet otherwise, he was suddenly like a young colt out to pasture. He recouped the energy of his youth, and went along on that level for another 20 years. He still amazes people. When he thinks he's tiring more readily, I tell him it's tough—he's only able to do the work of two young men instead of three, as he used to do.

I went with him to the Philippines and around the world. In India we met a missionary doctor who taught us more about B-vitamins. Back home, I was always looking for more energy to halfway keep up with Bart. I discovered *Prevention* magazine, which inspires me to like the foods I ought to like, and look with horror at all the foods dripping with empty calories, fat, salt, sugar, and white flour. Most physicians believe the magazine puts excessive emphasis on vitamin supplements, the value of which hasn't been proven in controlled tests. But it still has a lot to offer in inspiration and recipes. From it I learned about kelp, which is simply ground seaweed, rich in all minerals washed off the land into the sea. I also learned about lecithin, from soy beans, which helps dissolve the cholesterol in the blood. We still have to watch out for fats, but lecithin is a step in the right direction.

We add kelp and lecithin to our yeast dissolved in fruit juice. Bart calls it "gloop" and drinks it very fast along with his breakfast. He seldom reads anything about nutrition—he says that's my department. But he's convinced it works. He happily consumes the mountains of fruits and vegetables—without salt—that compose the bulk of our diet. He still succumbs at times to the home-baked goodies that other people serve him, but that's his option. Each of us makes our own choices. However, he now carefully distinguishes between foods "worth getting fat on" and those not worth it.

On the recommendation of a nutritionist in our area, we've started drinking distilled water. The rationale: distilled water is purified from all the bacteria, groundwater pollutants, chemicals, sediments from pipes of city water. Distilled water is "thirsty" water, able to soak up all the minerals and vitamins from the good foods we eat and distribute them to every cell in the body. The amount of minerals in ordinary tap water varies in different communities.

I have recently learned about complex carbohydrates in the form of vegetables and whole grains. These give even better results as the backbone of the diet than so much protein.

Some people would call us real crackpots on nutrition. We're satisfied that it's worth the trouble because it works. We rejoice in being able to work, travel, and enjoy life as much as we ever did.

As you can see, we didn't take on all these seemingly strange habits in one day. And if we really wanted to be more serious about all of this, we could go to the local nutritionist whose instructions I've read. We could get ourselves tested as to whether we're really getting or absorbing all the elements of diet we need. However, we feel really good, have no ailments. But maybe one of these days . . . .

The point is—learn what optimum nutrition is. Read books and magazine articles on the subject. Move in that direction step by step, as fast as you can take it emotionally or can change your tastes. I can promise you, your tastes will change. I enjoy eating now even more (if that's possible!) than I did when I ate sweets. An apple now tastes like a candy bar used to. My tastes for all flavors are sharpened. And leaving out salt is astonishingly easy. Vegetables taste sweet, and the subtle differences in flavor stand out.

You don't need to be one of those who says, "I'd rather die than eat that stuff." The trouble with that attitude is that you may not die. You may just become an invalid or develop chronic ailments.

You *can* change your tastes. "Set a guard over my mouth, O Lord; keep watch over the door of my lips" (Ps. 141:3, NIV). What you take into your mouth will, to a large extent, determine your health.

TEN 🙊:
REST AND EXERCISE—
Coping With Stress

Take rest; a field that has rested gives a bountiful crop.

Ovid, *Ars Amatoria,*
Book II, 1.35

Diet, important as it is, is only one leg of a three-legged stool on which physical health sits. The other two legs are rest and exercise. You need a balance of all three.

How late in life can a change of living pattern make a difference? Dr. Paul Parker says a person can turn back the clock 15 years by changing his lifestyle. "A typical patient I see is a man 55 years old, overweight, underexercised. He has high blood pressure, various complaints. I ask him to bring his wife in. We talk for a while. I encourage him, scare him, try to inspire him to change his pattern of living. His condition is not hopeless. He can actually turn himself around in three months. A man of 55 can be physiologically 70, or physiologically 40—a spread of 30 years, depending upon how he treats his body."

So far in this book we've been talking about beneficial stress—struggling, working, fighting to attain goals. But where do you get all that push?

Essentially, it's a mind-set. "Those who wait for the Lord will gain new strength; they will mount up with wings like eagles, they will run and not get tired, they will walk and not become weary" (Isa. 40:31). God the Creator never becomes tired, "He gives strength to the weary, and to him who lacks might He increases power. We can draw on God for spirit to keep on struggling, for courage to get up when we're down. (Isa. 40:29-30). "For in Him we live and move and have our being" (Acts 17:28, NIV). All that we're learning today about rest, exercise, and nutrition is only a rediscovery of principles written into God's creation in the first place.

In our society, average length of life is increasing, but so are chronic illnesses. More and more middle-aged and older Americans are suffering from persistent ailments, says Lois Verbrugge of the University of Michigan's Institute of Gerontology. She bases her study on an ongoing health survey of 300,000 people conducted annually by the National Center for Health Statistics, in suburban Washington, D.C. Heart disease and strokes are killing fewer, but affecting a greater number. Nonkiller diseases also, she found, were causing more lost days from work in the 45-64 age group. For example, upper gastrointestinal disorders were up 42 percent, arthritis up 27 percent, and gout 63 percent. Age 45 to 64 is young to be getting such things fastened on you. It's apparent we can't count on dying just before the ugly ailments arrive.

In the 18th century Montesquieu said, "Oh, the unhappy state of man! Scarcely has the mind reached full ripeness before the body begins to fall away." What can we do about our ailments?

We all need stress. Good stress is like ballast. We watched the oil tankers in Valdez, Alaska having the water pumped out before the oil from the Alaska Pipeline could be pumped in. They couldn't travel without the water—it was needed as ballast. We need work, hobbies, friends, goals to keep ourselves upright. People shrink, lose their balance from lack of stress. We all know of people who died shortly after retiring or entering a nursing home. At the same time, too much stress can sink the ship. The engines, the hold, the steering gear have to be strong enough to meet storms encountered along the way.

If we think we're carrying too heavy a load of cargo, too much stress, we must either increase our capacity for stress, or decrease the load. We can increase our capacity for stress by diet, exercise, and rest. We can eliminate unnecessary stresses like tobacco, alcohol, drugs, junk foods, sugar. We need reserve strength for unavoidable stresses like heat, cold, germs, change, special efforts or events.

Remember, stress is not in our environment, but in our reaction to our surroundings.

Bart and I have made a lifelong study of how to cope with stress. Jesus' advice: "Therefore do not be anxious for to-morrow; for tomorrow will care for itself. Each day has enough trouble of its own" (Matt. 6:34). You have to learn how to handle today's stress today. You don't have to drop out of life to survive.

Back in our 40s, Bart had a minibreakdown. For six weeks following my long bout with poor health, he suffered a near collapse—not surprisingly. He managed to preach, but spent all the rest of his time in bed. I brought books over from the church so he could study in bed. His secretary came over for dictation, or I relayed instructions to her. No one else really knew how bad he was, but we knew, and the doctor knew. And the doctor said, "The trouble with you people is you haven't learned how to carry your load."

We felt insulted. What callow lack of insight! Didn't he know we had an impossible load? But we never forgot his words. We went to work to learn how to carry our loads.

Rest

When you're down, there's nothing to do but rest. Rest, rest, and more rest. As much as you need. Cut the heroics, and see that you get the rest *you* need. As Bart told me so many times, "Stop worrying about being lazy, if you feel that bad, you are that bad. Stop worrying about the schedules other people keep. Figure out where you can be at equilibrium, and stick with it."

The world is not going to reward you for the number of hours you manage to sit upright at a desk. Or for the number of hours you rush around appearing busy. Even attending meetings, talking on the phone, going through motions won't do it. The world rewards you for what you accomplish. Look at your work in terms of results, and you can eliminate a lot of wasted effort.

We feel fortunate in the ministry to be more in control of our lives than a lot of people are. If it seems easier to study or work in bed, or in odd places and at odd hours, we can do it. We have concluded that it saves time off the job in the long-run to go to bed with a cold, so we go to bed with a cold. We've also figured out that if we feel utterly worn out, unable to face anything, in danger of coming down with the flu, we don't have to wait until we come down with the flu. We go to bed, and we won't get the flu. We don't even have to go away on vacation for a week to get a little extra rest. Just go to bed. It's astonishing how the hue of the world changes from indigo to rose when we do a little extra resting. A strategic retreat can mean recouping our forces for later advance.

One time I complained to a doctor, "I can't get over anything, even the slightest sore throat, without practically going to bed."

"Be glad," he said.

"Be glad of what?"

"Be glad that you can get over it. When I was in medical school, I became enormously impressed with the importance of rest—the power of the body to heal itself. When you rest, the energy that you normally direct to various activities is focused on your healing."

Yet many people in the ministry say they have no control over their lives, no time to themselves. Most people could control their lives a lot more than they do. My father, also a city pastor, trained himself to take one or two 20-minute naps during the day. He would just lie down clothed on a day bed, pull a cover over him and go to sleep.

Businessmen often say they can't take naps, that they have to work all day. But one man we know always napped for at least a half hour before he ate dinner. He too looked amazingly fresh. A school teacher says she likes to sleep when she gets home from teaching, for then she's good till midnight.

To rest most effectively, stay away from sleeping pills. After a few weeks the body overcompensates for the depressing effect and the pills actually stimulate against sleep. Several times I was unable to sleep from 2 A.M. on, and discovered I could still teach my class the next day. I felt OK till naptime, then slept deliciously, and was in good shape again for the evening. When you stop worrying about whether or not you sleep, you naturally sleep better. Authorities tell us that just lying relaxed in bed does your body almost as much good as sleeping.

To some people evenings are not as important as they are to us, and they prefer to go to bed early. A young and very gifted missionary who had hypoglycemia one time told me, "If I could get to bed at 9 o'clock, I'd feel OK. But I can't. There are just too many demands. Nobody else seems to need that much sleep."

A year or two after that, he caught an infectious disease and died. His remark about the rest he needed has haunted me.

As you get older, you experience loss of reserve capacity. You can't subject your body to prolonged stresses without bad results. But with extra rest, exercise, and good diet you can become strong enough to stand stress—for a short time. You don't need to fear stimulating stresses. It is better to be fully alive for fewer hours than half dead for more hours. Take control of your hours of rest.

Vacations and Hobbies

Along with daily rest, vacations and hobbies are important in combatting stress. We plan marvelous vacations and enjoy them to the full. But how could we enjoy our leisure so much if our whole life were leisure? It's the contrast between work and leisure that gives zest to both.

Another means of relaxing is to take minivacations. Have close at hand some hobbies that take you into another world instantly. I turn on the classical music station in our area for a quick getaway. Bart and I can sink into a magazine or book at the slightest opportunity. He likes to watch a baseball or football game on TV once in a while, and we occasionally manage to see an opera or concert or play. We love to walk in the woods and do so whenever possible.

> *Yet nature's charms—the hills and wood—*
> *The sweeping vales and foaming floods—*
> *Are free alike to all*
> (Robert Burns, "To Chloris")

"Each of you should learn to control his own body in a way that is holy and honorable" (1 Thes. 4:4, NIV). You don't need to become a victim to stress. If you want to enjoy good health as the years go on, learn how much rest you need, and your best pattern for rest. Come to terms with the fact that you may be different from other people. God has given you a certain maximum number of hours that you can function effectively. Even though He's given someone else another hour or two each day, don't let that wreck your health. Accept yourself and make the very most of the body you've been given. Learn how to carry your load.

Exercise

If you're tired, doesn't exercise just make you more tired? No. You need rest *and* exercise. Exercise can wake you up, make you feel refreshed and rested. Or it can leave you relaxed and ready to sleep. Fatigue from sedentary work can make you tense and unable to sleep. You won't sleep, specialists tell us, until your muscles are tired. So you need to keep exercise and rest in balance.

Why do you need to exercise? Way back in the time of the Roman Empire, Cicero discovered it was a good thing: "Exercise and temperance can preserve something of our early strength even in old age" (*De Senectute*, ch. 10, sec. 34). Diogenes, the Greek philosopher, said, "By constant exercise one develops freedom of movement—for virtuous deeds" (*Diogenes Laertius*, sec. 70). Shakespeare spoke of "the rich advantage of good exercise" (*King John*, act iv, sc. 2).

Our society has focused a lot of money and attention on spectator sports. College and professional sports center upon a few well-exercised athletes, while millions of people sit and watch them play. Ironically, several studies have shown that outstanding college athletes have a shorter than average life span.

So we're not talking about excelling in sports. We're

talking about exercise for the purpose of keeping your body in working order. A passion for personal fitness has swept the country. There's a minimum level of fitness necessary just to keep from deteriorating. Beyond that, you can work for whatever level of fitness you want. Most of us want the necessary level to do our work and enjoy life.

The President's Council on Physical Fitness has put out an excellent booklet, "Adult Physical Fitness." (This is for sale by the Superintendent of Documents, U.S. Government Printing Office, Washington, D.C. 20402.) It states:

> Physical fitness can be achieved at any age. You do not achieve it overnight. It does take effort. But the resulting feelings of well-being, renewed strength, and vitality are well worth the effort—and you can start on your way right now.

Kenneth Cooper's books *The New Aerobics* and *Aerobics for Women* also tell how to improve physical condition by gradually increasing exercise.

Fitness is defined as the ability of the individual to meet the demands of his environment. The body will adapt to whatever demands are placed upon it. When older people are confined to bed, they adapt—and become unable even to care for themselves. If you spend all your time sitting, you become unable to walk, lift a suitcase, carry groceries, or shovel snow. You can't meet the demands of your environment unless you exercise enough each day to be able to meet the occasional special stresses with ease.

Exercise increases the rate at which we process oxygen. We have more energy and our brains even work better. On the other hand, exercise relaxes. One investigation showed that a 15-minute walk is more effective in releasing tension than is a tranquilizer.

There's enormous satisfaction in having command of

your body. If you fail to exercise, your body becomes a hindrance instead of an instrument. Fitness means you can do whatever you want to—walk miles through airports, go up or down stairs, carry baggage when necessary, walk wherever you want to go for sight-seeing, climb monuments, walk up trails on mountains, run for short distances, stand when you have to. It means you can sweep, scrub, shovel, dig, or rake, as need requires.

Authorities in gerontology tell us that much of the stiffness, back pain, joint aches, and other discomforts of old age could be reduced if people would exercise regularly to maintain muscle tone and body flexibility. "Sit down and take it easy" is the worst possible advice for someone of any age, but especially for older people who need exercise most of all.

Robert N. Butler, expert on gerontology, says that exercise must be planned on a routine daily basis, that we simply must make time for it.

Even before the Fall, God provided man with exercise. Adam was to cultivate the garden and keep it (Gen. 2:15). Afterward, "God sent him out from the Garden of Eden, to cultivate the ground from which he was taken" (Gen. 3:23). Cultivation of the ground certainly required exertion.

People in Bible times didn't need to do exercises as such to keep in shape. They hiked over the hills as sheepherders. They pushed the plough, cut the grain with a scythe, and tied it in bundles. They trampled the juice from grapes. They beat the grain to thresh it, then tossed it up into the wind to separate the grain from the chaff. It took all the strength of two women to grind grain into flour. Women kneaded bread, gathered twigs, swept the house. Poor people gleaned grain left in the field by reapers. People fished by rowing a boat, throwing a net or line. They sawed, cut, pounded, did carpentry without benefit of power tools.

Today we wash clothes and dishes by pushing a button. We want the last word in electric brooms or vacuum cleaners. We wouldn't think of hanging our laundry or beating carpets.

But the body still needs exercise, so we have to manufacture movements for the body to make. Dr. Laurence E. Morehouse is a national authority on fitness. He has authored the sections on exercise and physical conditioning in various encyclopedias, including the *Encyclopaedia Britannica*. He worked out the exercise system used by the astronauts in Skylab. He says minimum maintenance for ordinary people can be achieved by five simple requirements everyday:

■ Limber up by reaching arms, twisting trunk, bending waist, and turning trunk.

■ Stand for a total of two hours during the day.

■ Lift something unusually heavy for five seconds.

■ Walk briskly for at least three minutes to stimulate your cardiovascular system.

■ Burn up 300 calories a day in physical activity.

In his book *Total Fitness*, Dr. Morehouse tells the why of exercise, and what it can do for you. He suggests many different activities for burning up those 300 calories a day. Walking three miles will do it, or you can jog the same three miles. Or you can work your 300 calories into the various activities of the day. But you have to move that much just to keep from deteriorating from lack of exercise. Standing is necessary to keep the blood vessels able to pump blood up to the heart. It also strengthens the bones. As with food, the beneficial effects of exercise cannot be stored, but must be renewed almost daily.

Charles Kuntzleman in his book *Diet Free!* (Rodale Press) explains how exercise can take weight off and keep it off. He suggests:

■ Use stairs instead of elevators.

■ Park your car at a distance and walk, instead of having it parked for you.
■ Bicycle to the store instead of driving.
■ Don't sit when you can stand, as when talking on the telephone.
■ Push a lawnmower instead of riding a tractor.
■ Hoist your snow with a shovel; clip your shrubbery with hand-clippers.
■ Do your housework and lawn work with brisk, vigorous movements.
■ Bend, reach, stretch, move as much as possible.

You'll feel better and look better. Line yourself up against a wall and stretch up to improve your posture—as many times a day as possible. Robert Butler quotes researcher Josef P. Hrachovec; "Exercise is the closest thing to an anti-aging pill now available. It acts like a miracle drug, and it's free for the doing."

Exercise helps to prevent strokes and also aids in recovery from them. It strengthens the heart, aids in preventing fatal heart attacks by developing auxiliary blood vessels to carry blood to and from the heart. It strengthens the heart after a heart attack. Doctors recommend exercise to maintain or recover movement for people with arthritis. Those with asthma or emphysema are better off if they exercise to improve what lung capacity they have. It's best to consult your doctor before embarking on an exercise program, especially where problems exist.

In recovering lost powers, it's always wise to make haste slowly. Start with whatever level of exercise you can manage, even if it's only walking for five minutes. Move on from there, a little bit more each day.

If you're badly out of shape, start with getting your pulse rate up to 150 minus your age. The average maximum for adults is 220 minus your age. If you are 50 years old and in poor condition, begin with exercise that brings your heartbeat up to 100 per minute. Gradually work up from there. If you are in good condition, you need to exercise at a pulse rate of at least 120 per minute to see any improvement.

The body needs three different kinds of exercise: stretching to keep limber, movements for increasing muscle strength, and steady exercise that gets the heartbeat up and thereby strengthens the heart and circulatory system. *Aerobics* refers to a variety of exercises which stimulate heart and lungs to deliver more oxygen to all parts of the body. Any activity that gets the heartbeat up to over 125 beats a minute and keeps it there for half an hour or more qualifies as an aerobic exercise. You can design your own pattern for exercise to meet these requirements.

The key to maintaining function, whether it's physical, mental, or social is, "Use it or lose it." You know what happens to muscles when an arm or a leg is in a cast for a broken bone to mend. The bone mends, but it takes months of working with those muscles to get back flexibility and strength. The same thing happens to your whole body if you don't use it.

Special exercise classes for older people have pitched their appeal at "rediscovering lost abilities." Some people claim that women of 60 can recover 95 percent of their original capacity for movement. Men can get back somewhat less, but their capacity was higher in the first place.

I think it's true. For three years I've been attending a once-a-week exercise class for all ages of women. Between classes I exercise for 20 minutes a day at home. I'm able to keep up with the average in the class. Some exercises aim at recovering the movements and positions of little children. It's amazing to realize that the capacity is still there. It really makes me feel young to do these things. When I push myself physically for a brief time each day, the rest of the time I can move with ease. Muscles are meant to be used. When not used, or not used enough, they deteriorate.

Bart and I enjoy our hour a day for exercise as a time of togetherness and refreshment. But we each exercise separately if we can't get together. In the summer we swim, in the spring and fall we walk or garden for an hour—rake leaves, dig, mow the lawn with a hand-mower. I add extra time for weeding or planting or trimming—to me, those activities are too mild to count as exercise. In the winter we walk—two or three miles a day, rain or sun, snow or ice. As a result, we enjoy shoveling snow when that's necessary, and do it with ease—for an hour. If we're not finished, we continue the next day.

We find exercise as addictive as any bad habit. We feel very upset if we miss even one day. We miss the high that exercise gives us, as well as the ability to sleep better.

If you look in the Bible for encouragement in taking care of the wonderful body God has given you, you'll find it. "I urge you, brothers, in view of God's mercy, to offer your bodies as living sacrifices, holy and pleasing to God. . . . Do not conform any longer to the pattern of this world, but be transformed . . ." (Rom. 12:1-2, NIV).

A person will certainly suffer for sins against his body, for lack of discipline in his physical habits. "The evil deeds of a wicked man ensnare him; the cords of his sin hold him fast. He will die for lack of discipline, led astray by his own great folly" (Prov. 5:21-23, NIV).

Map out your program for eating and exercise, and work toward it. "Watch and pray so that you will not fall into temptation. The spirit is willing, but the body is weak" (Matt. 26:41, NIV).

Have faith in your own capacity for self-discipline. The compliments you get, your own feeling of well-being will soon reinforce your efforts. Have faith that God will help you do what you really want to do. Your body is not your own; it was bought with a price. You can use your body as a precious gift that is given to you for awhile.

*E*LEVEN ✤:
CHANGE—
Can You Take It?

They must often change who would be constant in happiness or wisdom.

Confucius

Old age as a time of peace and serenity is a myth. Studies by gerontologists show that older persons experience more stresses than any other age group, and that these stresses are often devastating. What is remarkable is the strength of the aged to endure crisis. Some show amazing resilience. Yet others respond to trauma with depression, anxiety, psychosomatic illnesses, paranoia, and still others with garrulousness and irritability.

Bart's mother accepted the death of her husband of 45 years with amazing strength at the time. He collapsed with a cerebral hemorrhage one Sunday morning while visiting a Sunday School class of our church. She saw him to the hospital, then presented the message she was scheduled for.

Immediately afterward he died. We were away on vacation.

She did fine for a year. But when she came back to visit us the next summer, she was irascible, not her usual self at all. Somehow we understood that she was suffering through her loss again. After several months she became her old self and carried on triumphantly for a dozen more years.

Old age has the potential for being an immensely interesting and satisfying period of life. But this potential is threatened by many possibilities of loss and change. We can lose our health, suffer the death of people close to us. Crises loom—retirement, widowhood, major and minor illnesses. We must learn how to live with changes in physical appearance. Diminishing eyesight, hearing, sense of smell or taste threaten. Many experience decreased social status, some a drastically reduced standard of living.

Besides the changes which are part of the life cycle, our generation has seen vast modifications due to discoveries. We've seen the development of radio, television, nuclear power, space travel. We've benefited from amazing medical discoveries. All this takes adjustment. It's a different world from the one we started out in.

Old age itself means something entirely different today from what it used to. Within our memory, people who were 50 looked old, dressed old, talked old, acted old—were old. Today, most people of 50 feel they're getting into the prime of life. We're surprised but not shocked to see people of 73, 86, 95 traveling around the world, running governments, engaging in social service projects.

Is there a technique, an attitude, a quality of character that can enable us to deal with change constructively? Or are we like ships on the waves, tossed up and down by events? A lifetime of rich living should yield the ability to absorb change as it comes.

The eternal Christ is pictured in Revelation as having "head and hair . . . white like wool, as white as snow, and

His eyes were like blazing fire . . . Out of His mouth came a sharp double-edged sword. His face was like the sun shining in all its brilliance" (Rev. 1:14,16, NIV).

We associate white hair with age. Age means ripeness, completeness. Christ is young and old at the same time. As we grow in likeness to Him, we too can be young and old at the same time. We can carry with us the youth we had, overlaid and enriched with the fullness of the years. The sharp double-edged sword symbolizes the Word of God (Eph. 6:17). Knowledge of God's Word can give us the fresh edge we need to cut through all the traumas that can beset us.

Old age is neither inherently miserable nor inherently sublime. Rather, it's like any other stage of life—made up of problems, fears, joys, and potentials. It's part of the cycle of life—birth, childhood, maturity, decline, death. The old complete their life spans and make way for the young.

Yet it's a shock when the universal becomes true in ourselves. Studies show that few old people think of themselves as old. We are the same persons we have always been.

The challenge for young and old alike is to find peace in the midst of change. Jesus showed us how. "These things I have spoken to you, that in Me you may have peace. In the world you have tribulation, but take courage; I have overcome the world" (John 16:33). He spoke those words not in a snug academic atmosphere, but on the eve of His disgraceful trial and public death.

In this life the breathing times, the pauses in the battle, are only that. We know that the arrows of death, illness, unemployment, bereavement will fly. The only thing we don't know is whose life they will pierce at any given time.

Prepare for Change
How do you prepare for change? In the first place, give up

the idea that old age automatically brings peace and serenity. Don't plan on simply relaxing and enjoying the fruits of
your labors. Don't expect to arrive at some peaceful harbor
where you can tie up and stand still. You're going to have to
row all the way. Even an invalid must struggle to stay on
top. The storms of life present a continuing challenge.

Joshua warned the Israelites about to enter the Promised
Land, "You have not passed this way before. . . . Con-
secrate yourselves, for tomorrow the Lord will do wonders
among you." They were to follow along after the Ark of the
Covenant, "that you may know the way by which you shall
go" (Josh. 3:4-5).

None of us has traversed the whole way yet, but we can
learn from those farther along in the journey. We can learn
what to take for the trip, and what to leave behind.

In 1983, Bart and I hosted a trip to China. The China
International Travel Service controls all travel in the People's Republic of China. Ahead of time they warned us in
their brochure that it was a strenuous trip. I urged the people going with us to get in shape by walking several miles
each day. Travelers who'd gone before warned us of primitive hotel conditions, strange food, heat and cold, the
drabness of Chinese dress. They told us to dress for comfort,
not style. When we got there, people on the tour were glad
to be equipped and in shape for strenuous walks and climbs
and long hours on the go. Most things turned out better
than expected, but it helped to have been warned.

In the United States massive efforts are directed to pre-
paring the young for adult roles. In contrast, very little is
done to prepare adults for old age. We have to prepare
ourselves, by listening and learning from those who've gone
before.

We can prepare for the changes of old age by realizing it's
not a steady state beginning at age 65. Some gerontologists
divide old age into early old age, 65 to 74; advanced old

age, 75 and above. Dr. Robert Butler says that a realistic view is more flexible, taking actual capacities into account. Some people in their 90s are still in early old age. They haven't yet declined noticeably. And some people in their 30s are already old.

We can prepare for the changes of old age by expecting a different perception of time. The years seem to go faster and faster. To a 2-year-old, one year is forever, a space of time beyond imagining. To a 10-year-old, it's a long time, one-tenth of his life. To a 70-year-old, a year whips by.

Furthermore, the freshness of childhood experiences make time seem longer. A child's year is filled with a multitude of new experiences, each of them strongly written in his consciousness. To a 70-year-old, so much is routine that few things stand out as memorable. This sense of time whizzing by can make traumas seem to come one on top of another, when actually they may be years apart.

The older person can slow down this sense of time by taking on new experiences. Travel makes time slow down because it's packed with new experiences. Seen in retrospect, each day stretches out into a long progression of events.

We can prepare for change by broadening our interests, enriching our inner resources. Those who study old age tell us that people do not change their basic pattern of living even after they retire. Their interests, activities, associations, and relationships are formed during earlier years of life. The setting may change, but not the activities or patterns themselves. Few develop new interests in their later years. They draw on the resources they already have to meet inevitable changes. Busy people remain busy. Uninvolved people remain uninvolved.

We can prepare for change by learning how to handle leisure. Studies show that in spite of all our labor-saving devices, hours of work for the average person have decreased little. Husbands hold second jobs, wives work full-time plus carrying home responsibilities. Decreased quality and increased cost drive many to do-it-yourself jobs. So the actual free time gained in the past 100 years doesn't add up to more than two or three hours per week. People have no preparation for the enforced leisure of retirement.

To prepare more effectively for changes ahead, we might become less intent on acquiring and doing, and more intent on learning and being.

What does last to the end of life is man's potential for growth. Old age need not be thought of as a stage of stagnation. We don't need to accept habits and prejudices as set at any age. We have no need to demand that people cater to our prejudices and eccentricities because we're old. We can keep on growing and changing to the end of life.

> Does the road wind uphill all the way?
>   Yes, to the very end.
> Will the day's journey take the whole long day?
> From morn to night, my friend.
>   (Christina Rosetti, "Uphill")

Whether later life is uphill or downhill depends upon your conception of its purpose. If life is only physical, it's obviously downhill from age 20 on. If life is essentially spiritual, it's uphill all the way. Even the direst changes can add up to spiritual growth.

If we can redistribute learning, work, and leisure throughout life, we can grow till the very end. It's tragic to assume that education is for youth, work for the middle years, leisure for old age.

The old need to share in the work of the world for their own sake as well as for others. And they need to learn that even undesirable changes bring new opportunities for learning and growth. Older people need to keep their intellectual and spiritual appetites sharp, their curiosity alive.

Ample evidence shows that older people can change if they want to. Even those who have aged unhappily, giving in to weakness and emptiness, can develop new attitudes. They can find other ways to get attention than dwelling on bodily disfunctions and complaints.

We can prepare for the changes of old age by developing good mental health. We can work out problems of relationships, thereby learning. We can deal with problems left over from childhood instead of shoving them under the carpet of work and busyness. Psychiatrists tell us that problems of childhood often return to haunt the old person. Impressions received in childhood are so vivid they can never be erased. But they can, by the grace of God, be faced and worked through. Conflicts that are merely repressed generally emerge later. They come to the surface all too easily in old age when the barriers are down because of illness or bereavement.

We can work toward good mental health by finding and being our real selves, not hiding behind the personages others expect us to be. We can develop the habit of looking for the rainbow, the beauty that can emerge after the storm.

We can prepare for the changes of old age by learning the art of contentment. "I have learned to be content in whatever circumstances I am" (Phil. 4:11). Contentment is a matter of habit. "He who is of a calm and happy nature will hardly feel the pressure of age, but to him who is of an opposite disposition youth and age are equally a burden" (Plato, *Republic*, bk. I, 329-D).

Hold to the Unchanging
In coping with change, first of all hold to the unchanging. There can be only one center for our lives that never changes—"I, the Lord, do not change" (Mal. 3:6). "Jesus Christ is the same yesterday and today, yes and forever"

(Heb. 13:8). Jobs, income, and people move in and out of our lives, but He's always there. We dare not forego a living relationship with the one Person we can count on forever.

Human relationships will all come to an end. Even with the most ideal friendship or marriage, one person will die first. We must live in a balance between giving ourselves in intimacy and remembering the possibility of loss.

"All flesh is like grass, and all its glory like the flower of grass. The grass withers, and the flower falls off, but the Word of the Lord abides forever" (1 Peter 1:24). Physical life passes as quickly as grass withers. Our paltry accomplishments, so lovely at the time, drop off like flower petals. But God and His Word last forever. We'd better stake our real trust on what's going to last.

Keep Some Things the Same

We can learn to face change. Yet at the same time part of us cries out for as many things as possible that don't change. Loss of a husband or wife comes as a terrible trauma. "It's like having part of yourself cut off," said my mother when newly widowed. The worst thing you can do at such a time is to change everything else in your life. Wait. Stay in the same house if you can until you can make up your mind what to do. Hold onto your friends. Continue in the same routine. That alone can help get you through.

At 50, we struggle with the idea of remaining in the same house or job for the rest of our lives. At 70, we typically cling to the familiar. We like to go to a different place for each vacation—but we want to come back to the same house and job. I don't even want to change the furnishings or pictures or the colors.

People who must change their residence find it helps to be able to take their own furnishings and keepsakes. Each thing we have collected over a lifetime represents a family heirloom, or some marvelous bargain acquired with great effort or energy. Or some treasure dearly bought in a far place. Or some gift thoughtfully given by a loved one. I don't want to throw all that out and start over.

Many of us don't even want to undergo the stress of small changes. When I read Alvin Toffler's book, *Future Shock*, I understood why. All of us have our adaptive limits. Why waste adaptive energy on unimportant changes? The human organism simply breaks down physically and psychologically under the stress of too many changes, too many decisions.

After I read that, I went out and bought a bedspread exactly like the one that was wearing out. I'd worked out my color scheme, that particular style of bedspread fit, and I didn't want to change.

Barzillai, "a very old man" of 80, refused David's invitation to come to Jerusalem and live at court. "Let your servant return," he said to David, "that I may die in my own town near the tomb of my father and mother" (2 Sam. 19:37, NIV). His attitude was typical of that of most older people. He didn't want to give up the familiarity of home even to live at court.

Know When to Fight

When change is thrust upon you, you can't keep things the same. When should you fight change? When should you yield without a fight? It is important to distinguish between things that can be changed and those that cannot. In regard to retirement, people usually have little choice. If you do have a choice, exercise it. Bart and I have opted not to retire, until a change in health or other circumstances requires it.

The death of a loved one affords us no choice. Yet some people fight bereavement with denial, anger, protest, or blame—all unhealthy reactions.

We may have a choice about our own health. We can

decide to fight for health, to give way to natural decline only after a hard-fought delaying action. Or we can wallow in ailments that could be prevented. Don't accept illness without a fight. You can quite often win.

You may have a choice about moving to another locality, or another house. Some are revitalized with a change of scene. Others are shattered.

A 92-year-old woman living alone fought so hard for her independence that she refused any assistance. She failed to realize that accepting a little help would make real independence possible longer.

We must ask God constantly to help us change the things that can be changed, and to accept the things that cannot be changed.

We can fight sensory decline by accepting extensions and substitutions for our own powers. Think of the blessings of modern dental work, glasses, hearing aids, pacemakers, walkers, even wheelchairs. B.F. Skinner's book, *Enjoy Old Age,* gives an excellent catalog of suggestions for fighting the disabilities of advancing years. It's wrong to accept these losses without a fight—you'll sink into yourself if you do.

We all fight changes in appearance in different ways. I'm all for the delaying action of nutrition and exercise, but I draw the line there. Others get a lift from a new hair color or a face-lift.

An article in *Vogue* magazine discussed "Youth & Beauty, Age & Wisdom":

Many women, myself included, are actually looking forward to life on the other side of youth and beauty. Reports filtering back from friends who have already begun looking like their mothers are very favorable. Reports from the mothers themselves are enthusiastic. These women are discovering that age and wisdom can be very appealing alternatives.

(Mary Kay Blakely, November 1981,
Courtesy *Vogue*, ©1981
by Conde Nast Publications, Inc.).

Acceptance, Not Blame

After we've fought as hard as we can, or even while still fighting, there comes a time to accept. We have to learn to accept the unexpected as an opportunity. Complications are the spice of life. We all need challenge. People who try to make life simple often succeed in making it sterile. A life without problems could be deadly in its boredom. Youth usually has the resilience to absorb trouble and go on. We maintain the spirit of youth if we do likewise.

The Book of Job teaches us that Satan can afflict a believer only to the degree that God allows. The Bible as a whole shows God's providence. God is in control. So we with Job have to accept whatever happens as part of God's plan for us. "Though He slay me, yet will I trust Him" (Job 13:15, NKJV).

Job learned what could be gained from loss and suffering. "But He knows the way I take; when He has tried me, I shall come forth as gold" (Job 23:10). We can greet evil things that come our way with the closed fist of bitterness, or with the open hand of acceptance. We can thank God for letting us experience the years of old age, with their inevitable losses. The last years constitute a training ground for eternity. "The time has arrived for pruning the vines" (Song 2:12). God doesn't punish those He loves, He prunes and disciplines them for greater growth and productivity. "Those whom the Lord loves He disciplines" (Heb. 12:6). As we open our hands and give what has been taken away, we relax in trust. Relinquishment is a spiritual law of life.

It's part of God's plan. The later years constitute a time of pruning and preparation for heaven.

Whatever happens, don't blame anyone. Paul, imprisoned in Rome, wrote that his confinement had turned out for the greater progress of the Gospel (Phil. 1:12-14). From the cross, Jesus said of the very people who had caused His agony, "Father forgive them; for they do not know what they are doing" (Luke 23:34). Joseph, as viceroy of Egypt, said to his brothers, "Now do not be grieved or angry with yourselves, because you sold me here; for God sent me before you to preserve life. . . . Now, therefore, it was not you who sent me here, but God" (Gen. 45:5, 8). We only make a bad situation worse by looking for someone to blame for our troubles.

Look for the Compensations

However bad things are, we can look for the compensations. During the months I spent totally at home, caring for our daughter Janet, I found little joys, little compensations. She needed my whole attention, yet couldn't stand much excitement. We spent evening after evening together watching the fire burn in the fireplace. A fire is never two minutes the same. It leaps about, it's alive, it turns different colors, it's ever doing something different. For the first time in my life, I got enough of watching a fire.

Never before that spring was I so aware of tulips coming up. Janet and I walked in the snow, we dug in the yard. She had just graduated from college with honors, but now she needed to do little quiet things. I had to slow down and content myself.

I learned to thank the Lord for new little blessings every morning. "Because of the Lord's great love we are not consumed, for His compassions never fail. They are new every morning; great is Your faithfulness" (Lam. 3:22-23, NIV). Jeremiah, in his grief over Jerusalem, found consolation for his grief: "The Lord is my portion; . . . I will wait for Him" (Lam. 3:24, NIV). After eight months, Janet was able to go back to work.

God asks us to use every opportunity to grow. Enforced leisure in later years can give the chance to do things we've always claimed we wanted to do.

All our lives we're told, "Don't live in the past, don't live in the future, live in the present." Only after many decades do we learn this, but we do learn it. We learn to enjoy each day for itself—because we don't know how many more we'll have. "You must reach old age before you can understand the meaning—the splendid, absolute, unchallengeable, irreplaceable meaning of the word *today*!" (Claudel, *Journal*) We learn increasingly to find joy in the very act of living. Going on errands, cooking a meal, tidying up—all seem newly enjoyable to me, a part of being alive.

For some, old age is a time of harvest, of reaping benefits from investments of earlier years. Bart and I have a constantly accumulating cache of color slides of our travels in the basement. He takes the pictures, most of them very good, has them developed, brings them home. I let the bag of slides sit around for a while, then take it to the basement—unviewed. The last few years neither of us seems to have time to look over pictures, let alone organize them. Often we're busy planning the next trip. When we get old, we tell ourselves, we'll settle down and look at our pictures.

A friend of ours made a great hobby of entertaining and keeping in touch with friends. Now very limited physically, she's having a great time traveling around the country visiting the friends she helped so much in the past. Letting them do for her now is like taking income from her investments.

Look for the Open Door
Besides looking for the little joys, we can come to grips with the big question, "Why has God left me here?" Why, after the death of husband, wife, or children? Why, after the loss

of work that I loved? Why, after the loss of health?

People have found many different answers to that hard question. Some in the nursing homes find other patients they can minister to. Others find a new kind of work, a second family in those who need them.

Some find their answer in simply being, living close to God. They become a benediction to the people around them, to loved ones who care for them. When Moses came down from that mountain, he didn't know that his face shone from speaking with God. The benediction of such a person's presence may be unconscious. We can all aim at being what God wants us to be in all circumstances.

"Trust in the Lord with all your heart, and do not lean on your own understanding; in all your ways acknowledge Him, and He shall direct your paths" (Prov. 3:5-6, NKJV). From the time I discovered that verse at about age 27, I've generally felt pretty sure of what God wanted me to do next. It wasn't always what I wanted to do, but pursuing His path always turned out to be exactly right. I've learned He never closes one door without opening others. When the end of this life comes into sight, our work for Him seems all the more urgent.

Jesus said, "We must work the works of Him who sent Me, as long as it is day; night is coming when no man can work" (John 9:4).

God offers His open door to every one of us. It's up to us to walk through it.

TWELVE ❧
DEATH—
The Last
Great Adventure

Death's but a path that must be trod,
If man would ever pass to God.

Thomas Parnell,
A Night Piece on Death, 1.67

Going on a trip involves a lot of preparation. So does dying. In either case, if you don't accept the fact that you're going, you can't get ready.

Recently, Bart and I traveled to Hawaii. Getting ready to go proved extremely difficult. We had been overjoyed to have all our children home for Christmas. One family was here a week before Christmas, everybody—15 in all—here for three days over Christmas, and another family stayed through New Year's.

Before that I'd been working on this book up to the last possible moment, not to speak of getting ready for Christmas. Two days after New Year's I taught one of my classes, then found I had to go to bed with a cold or I'd never be able to travel by air on January 7. Bart taught my second class and that threw him off balance for getting his affairs in order for leaving.

So on the last day we were both working like mad getting commitments to other people in shape to leave, packing, making arrangements for the house. That day I didn't have the slightest desire to go to Hawaii. But Bart was expected as chaplain on the cruise ship taking us from island to island, so we had to go.

I thought, "If either of us didn't like travel, this would be a time when we would be screaming at each other, 'What in the world are we torturing ourselves like this for? Why do we even try to do such things?'"

But I remembered other stressful departures, and I knew how much we'd enjoy the trip once we were off. Neither of us said a word. We just flew around working till at last we had everything in order, bags packed, alarm set. Then we could go to bed and sleep in peace. But we had to face the fact that we were going, in order to get through that day.

All of us have to accept the reality that we will die sometime or soon. If we don't accept death as a fact of life, we won't be prepared to go. We won't enjoy life as much either. We'll miss the joy of the journey of going home to be with the Lord. We won't help our family and friends to prepare for our departure. And not accepting death won't change the fact. We'll still die.

Paul likened death to a journey: "The time of my departure has come" (2 Tim. 4:6).

Make Your Reservations

In taking a trip, we like to make arrangements well ahead of time. We may make reservations ourselves, or choose a travel agent, decide on a guide, and make a down payment. I had thought for many years it would be nice to go to

Hawaii, but I never would have gotten there if I hadn't become more definite than that.

The Bible tells us how to make a reservation for heaven. Jesus said:

> "He who hears My word, and believes Him who sent Me, has eternal life, and does not come into judgment, but has passed out of death into life" (John 5:24).

> "He who believes in the Son has eternal life; but he who does not obey the Son shall not see life, but the wrath of God abides on him" (John 3:36).

> "For this is the will of My Father, that everyone who beholds the Son, and believes in Him, may have eternal life" (John 6:40).

Any citizen or resident of the United States can go to Hawaii without a passport. We can settle having the right citizenship for heaven right now with God, through believing and obeying Jesus Christ. It's open to everyone who does so. "For our citizenship is in heaven," (Phil. 3:20). If you don't live in the United States, you can apply for a passport to go to Hawaii. But you won't get into any country or kingdom in this world, let alone the next, without having the requirements for entry in order.

For any difficult trip, you need a guide. We wanted to see all the islands of Hawaii, and thought a cruise would be the easy way. The captain would get us there. We've found we see more in the Holy Land by following a guide.

God offers us Himself as a Guide through death. "Even though I walk through the valley of the shadow of death, I fear no evil; for Thou art with me" (Ps. 23:4). If we have our passports or citizenship in order, reservations made, Guide chosen, Christ will deliver us from slavery to the fear of death, to which some are subject all their lives (Heb. 2:15).

And He'll go before us to work out all necessary arrangements. "In My Father's house are many dwelling places . . . I go to prepare a place for you." He said He would come again for us, and take us to be with Himself. We don't even need to worry about how to get there, He'll be the Guide. "I am the way, the truth, and the life; no one comes to the Father, but through Me." (John 14:2-6).

Learn All You Can
After Bart and I have made our reservations for a trip, we like to learn as much as possible about the place we're going to. We talk to people, read books and articles. That's a good idea with heaven too. The Bible tells us something about it, though it doesn't have nearly as much to say about heaven as it does about money and treating our fellowmen properly. It tells us all we need to know about getting to heaven, but precious little about what it's really like. Probably it would be too wonderful for us to cope with. We'd all want to go right now. Recently I heard a minister pray, "Lord, forgive us for wanting heaven before we get there."

If you want to get really inspired about how wonderful death is, read Maurice Rawlings, *Beyond Death's Door.* That book makes me sometimes want heaven right now. Dr. Rawlings is a cardiologist who often brings patients back from short-term clinical death. For some the "death" experience is so terrible they beg him to get them "out of hell." For others, it's so wonderful they don't want to come back.

From the time we enter this world, our personal identity and survival seem supremely important to us. We're shocked at the passage of time, since we can't believe this little life is passing so quickly. God has set eternity in our hearts (Ecc. 3:11). Nature offers us many object lessons of hope. The death of winter awakens to new life in the spring. The seed is buried and dies, to spring up again in new life (1 Cor. 15:35-58). The baby coming out of the womb must suffer a sense of crisis, of trauma, of dying.

The dragonfly begins as a grub in water. At the right time it surfaces, finds its wings, and flies away. The ones left in the water might wonder where it went and why it doesn't return. It can't go back because it has wings now.

The butterfly emphasizes to us the idea of this struggle as it breaks loose from the cocoon to enter a new dimension of living.

The Bible speaks of death as if it were simply going from one room to another. "You shall go to your fathers in peace" (Gen. 15:15). Death is "going the way of all the earth" (Josh. 23:14). Hezekiah, after his illness and recovery, wrote, "Like a shepherd's tent my dwelling is pulled up and removed from me; as a weaver I rolled up my life" (Isa. 38:12). Paul said that being absent from the body means being at home with the Lord (2 Cor. 5:8). He preferred going, but was willing to stay for the sake of others (Phil. 1:23-24).

Paul considered that the sufferings of this present time are not worthy to be compared with the glory that is to be revealed to us (Rom. 8:18).

He said that eye has not seen, nor ear heard, all that God has prepared for those who love Him. Yet these things are revealed through the Spirit (1 Cor. 2:9-10).

Decide What to Take

When we're hosting a tour, people always ask, "What will I need? What kind of clothes shall I take?" They want to know a year ahead of time, so they can plan their wardrobes. I always make a list of what I'll need. In the case of heaven, God provides the clothing we'll need—"He has clothed me with garments of salvation, He has wrapped me with a robe of righteousness" (Isa. 61:10). So we don't need to pack any clothes at all. If we don't have the garments He provides, nothing else will do.

But some things will automatically go along with us to heaven. "For we must all appear before the Judgment Seat of Christ, that each one may be recompensed for his deeds in the body, according to what he has done, whether good or bad" (2 Cor. 5:10). So we'd better study out Christ's commandments for this life. "Blessed are the dead who die in the Lord . . . that they may rest from their labors, for their deeds follow with them" (Rev. 14:13).

We learn more about rewards and losses from deeds done in this life from the Apostle Paul (1 Cor. 3). There are deeds that we can take along and others that will be burned up. In heaven, we will rest from our labors. All toil, tears, sweat, strain will be left behind. What will remain is whatever we have accomplished for Christ.

How Much Does It Cost?
Besides other preparations for a trip, you have to come up with enough money. Even after the basic trip is paid for people always ask, "How much extra will I need—or want?" So they buy travelers checks, take along cash or charge cards.

For the journey to heaven, Jesus is the way. He has paid for the passage. But we can convert some of the money of earth into the currency of heaven. It will go along with us. Jesus said, "Do not lay up for yourselves treasures upon earth, where moth and rust destroy, and where thieves break in and steal. But lay up for yourselves treasures in heaven" (Matt. 6:19-20). Giving to the Lord's work is like setting up a bank account in a foreign country. We are converting the currency of earth into the currency of heaven. Some people like to let their money work for the Lord after they're gone by putting contributions to Christian organizations in their wills.

Countdown for Heaven

Every trip involves a last-minute countdown—a checklist of things that must be done before departure. We must leave the key with someone, engage people to mow the grass, shovel snow, or check on the house. We have to pay our bills, stop the milk or newspaper, leave our address with loved ones.

Accepting the fact that we're going to die gives us time to get ready to go. "Set your house in order, for you shall die and not live," said the Lord to Hezekiah through Isaiah (Isa. 38:1). My mother even went through attic, closets, and basement to clear out clutter. She felt the Lord was going to call her soon because of a heart condition.

The final countdown—the trauma preceding death—isn't always pleasant. It may be quite agonizing. But a difficult departure may be necessary for our complete preparation. And we can't enjoy the glorious moment of take-off to the full unless everything is completely in order.

We all want to leave various things behind. Remember how Dorcas "was abounding with deeds of kindness and charity, which she continually did." After she was gone, the widows stood with Peter and showed "all the tunics and garments which Dorcas used to make while she was with them" (Acts 9:36-39).

We all want to leave some works that others will cherish. We may want our children to have certain keepsakes from us. Or we may be able to leave something more substantial.

By far the biggest thing we can leave is the example of a godly life. We'd like to be like Abel, who "through faith, though he is dead, he still speaks" (Heb. 11:4).

We want time to put our legacies in order. Remember how Elijah, when he knew God was going to take him, said to Elisha, "Ask what I shall do for you before I am taken from you" (2 Kings 2:9). Because they could talk about it, Elijah was able to pass on his mantle to Elisha. We do our loved ones a favor if we can talk things over, answer their questions while it's still possible.

Just before she died, Bart's mother gave herself to encouraging him. "Don't feel bad for me," she said, "I'm going to a wonderful place and I want to go, I'm ready. You carry on in the Lord's work, and remember, the separation won't be for long." Her words have been an enormous comfort to Bart.

People want to leave many different kinds of legacies, intellectual, spiritual, material, and even physical. Some want to give their bodies for research or organ transplants after death.

There comes a sense of completion when everything is in order. Jesus said, "It is finished!" (John 19:30) Paul said, "I have fought the good fight, I have finished the course, I have kept the faith" (2 Tim. 4:7). People of every stage of life have availed themselves of the victory over death possible in Christ.

Yet others fit Thoreau's description all too well: "How earthy old people become—mouldy as the grave! Their wisdom smacks of the earth. There is no foretaste of immortality in it. They remind me of earthworms and mole crickets" (Journal—Aug. 16, 1853).

Even some Christians deny to the very end, and leave their loved ones totally unprepared. Open communication ahead of time can fortify loved ones for their grief.

On Your Way!
When we have a trip in prospect, people quite often ask me, "Are you excited?" I have to answer quite honestly, "I haven't really had time to get excited. There's so much to do before going."

But there's one moment that never fails to stir me with

excitement and anticipation. That's the moment of starting off in the car, or taking off in the plane. Everything's been done that can be done—now it's off into the wild blue yonder.

I saw my mother take off for heaven in the same spirit of anticipation. She had already taught me so much about how to live. At the end she showed me how to die beautifully.

I was in Detroit when my brother-in-law called saying she was in the hospital with a serious heart attack. She had lived alone after my father's death, and often assured us that we needn't worry about her. She had prayed about it, and trusted God that she'd be able to summon help if she needed it. When her final heart attack came, she was able to get to the phone and summon a neighbor who was a doctor. He found her slumped on the floor and got her to the hospital.

By a series of small miracles, I arrived in time. Though I had to catch two planes from Detroit to Waterloo, Iowa, I was there in just five hours from the moment of that phone call.

I found my mother in the hospital connected up with oxygen tubes and apparatus, struggling hard for breath. She opened her eyes and asked me to read Psalm 121: "I lift up my eyes to the hills. From whence does my help come? My help comes from the Lord, who made heaven and earth." (vv. 1-2, RSV)

"Yes, that's it." I held her hand and prayed aloud, committing her to God's care. I asked that she have assurance every moment. I prayed that if she was to go or stay she would feel completely in the hollow of His hand.

Mother said, "I know that. I've lived by it all my life. 'For me to live is Christ, and to die is—' " she faltered.

" 'Gain,' " I finished for her. "You remember when I was sick in the hospital that time? It looked to me like the simplest thing in the world to step over into the next world."

"I'm glad you came back that time," she said.

At midnight Mother announced matter-of-factly, "I'm going soon now." I recited John 14:1-3:

Let not your heart be troubled;
believe in God, believe also in Me
In My Father's house are many dwelling places;
if it were not so, I would have told you;
for I go to prepare a place for you.
And if I go and prepare a place for you,
I will come again, and receive you to Myself;
that where I am, there you may be also.

"You're going to a wonderful place, Mother."

"I know that," she said. "But why can't I get there? Why is it so hard?"

I repeated the 23rd Psalm, accidentally omitting one phrase.

"My cup overflows," Mother interrupted, correcting me. "It's only a few steps more. Why can't I get there? Take these things off, and let me go." She was pulling at the oxygen tube, trying to throw off the covers and leave the bed. "Why are they keeping me here? I want to go." We held her gently.

"No—it's all right," she said. With a sigh of resignation she let the nurse arrange the oxygen tube again. "Psalm," she gasped. I read.

My sister thanked her for being a good mother. She smiled a little. Tears streaming down our faces, I said, "You're almost there, Mother, and it's going to be wonderful. The separation will be only for a little while."

She looked at us. "Yes. Only for a little while." Then she lapsed into unconsciousness and soon was gone from us.

But in that room was a great sense of arrival, of accomplishment, like that of childbirth. She was free of the crumpled body on the bed. The pain was over. Part of me was now in heaven.

We took care of arrangements, then went out into the night. It was 3 A.M.

Our family get-together after the funeral was a festive occasion. Before her coronary Mother had put up a Christmas tree. Her refrigerator was stocked and her friends brought in additional food. People told me what she had meant to them as aunt, neighbor, friend, spiritual mother. We talked of her acts of kindness and of love.

All this was 26 years ago. But she, being dead, yet speaks.

Are you ready for that last glorious adventure? Paul referred to his departure in the Greek as *analusis* (2 Tim. 4:6). It was the philosopher's word for solving problems, mysteries. "For now we see in a mirror dimly, but then face to face (1 Cor. 13:12). When we arrive in heaven, all mysteries will be made plain.

It was the sailor's word for unloosing the ropes that bound a ship to the wharf. Remember Tennyson's poem, "Sunset and evening star, And one clear call for me . . ." He saw death as a loosing from his moorings, a going out to sea, an opportunity to meet his Pilot face to face. "When I have crossed the bar." *Analusis* was the farmer's word for unhitching the donkey or ox from his harness at close of day, letting him go free to feed and rest. It was the soldier's word for untying his tent ropes in the morning and getting off on the march.

It was the traveler's word for taking off on a journey. As Christians we need to be always ready, with passport in hand, bags packed, ready to go. Just as the trauma of departure is forgotten in the joy of the trip, so it will be at death. By faith we can look forward to our last great adventure.